Content

Volume 96:4 Winter 2006/7

Poems

5	Michael Longley	Call
		Horseshoe
		Lullaby
		Cygnus
		Cloudberries
9	David Harsent	The Hut In Question
		from Broken Glass
12	Eavan Boland	How It Was Once In Our Country
13	Seán Ó Ríordáin	My Mother's Burial
15	John Fuller	Pomme
18	Omar Sabbagh	Vital
19	Semyon Lipkin	Charred
20	Ruth Padel	The Peaks, The Troughs
		As I Flick Off The Remote In The Gulf I Think
		Of An Ancient Greek Playwright
24	Glyn Maxwell	Flags And Candles
		Kaspar Hauser
26	E. A. Markham	The Story Of A Revolution
27	Alan Brownjohn	Ludbrooke: His Compliment
		His Chivalry
		His Pride
		His Red
		His Physique
30	John Fuller	The Dance
31	Krystyna Miłobędzka	(how to make a star)
32	David Morley	The Charges On Midsummer Night For
		The Coventry Mysteries
33	Yang Lian	Home
34	Greg Delanty	The Naming Of Clouds
35	Jackie Kay	Darling
36	Alan Jenkins	At The Grave Of Joseph Brodsky
40	Shi Tao	*from* Dedicated To The Book Of The Dead
42	Amanda Aizpuriete	That Would Probably Be Best
		Dat Wid Laekly Be Best
44	Marie Étienne	*from* Some Of Them Are Japanese

47	Alison Brackenbury	On A February Night
48	Julia Casterton	Goblins
49	Sean Borodale	Lyrigraph For A Lady Chatting (From Reading To Bath By Train)

Centrefold

53	Glyn Maxwell	*'Before, Behind, Between, Above, Below':* The Poem That Became A Novel That Became A Play
61	*Musarum Sacerdos*	An Interview With Michael Longley
65	Alec Peever	*Down To The Letter*
66	Introductions to *Back In Print:*	Ruth Fainlight
		Peter Porter
		Penelope Shuttle
		Jeffrey Wainwright on Geoffrey Hill
72	C.L. Dallat	*Company Of Loners: The* Workshop Gen *Poets*

Reviews

79	Adam Thorpe on Michael Longley
82	Jay Parini on Robertson's Tranströmer and Paterson's Rilke
86	David Morley on Alan Brownjohn
88	Steven Matthews on reissued anthologies by Crawford and Muldoon
91	Todd Swift on Paul Farley
93	Patrick McGuinness on W.N.Herbert
95	Paul Batchelor on Lorna Goodison, Philip Levine and Dunya Mikhail
98	Michael Hulse on Justin Quinn, Andrew McNeillie, Paul Batchelor and Andrew Grieg
101	Michael Longley The Holly Bush *i.m Dorothy Molloy*
102	Patrick Crotty on Dorothy Molloy and Seán Dunne
105	Graham Hartill on Frances Presley, Gael Turnbull and Elaine Randell
109	Giles Goodland on Owen Sheers, Vernon Watkins and Dannie Abse
111	Charlotte Newman on Patrick Lane and Mitsuo Takahashi
114	Ruth Fainlight The Yellow Plate *i.m. Assia Gutman*
116	Margaux Poueymirou briefs on the new biography of Assia Wevil

Endpapers

119	Chris Holifield	*Letter From Tavistock Place*
121	Editorial	
122	Lemn Sissay	*News From The Beat*
124	Frank Dullaghan	The Royal Academy
125	Letter to the Editor	
125	Again, Please!	
127	Contributors	

28842

This book is due for return on or before the last date shown below.

Consider the kind of body that enters blueness...
—Eavan Boland

Michael Longley
Call

Alone at Carrigskeewaun for the millennium
My friend sits at the hearth keeping the cottage warm.
Is it too late to phone him? Is it midnight yet?
That could be me, a meadow pipit calling out.
Otters are crossing from Dooaghtry to Corragaun.
There are mallards and widgeon and teal for him to count.
Three dolphins are passing the Carricknashinnagh shoal.
He has kept for this evening firewood that is very old.
Bog deal's five thousand years make the room too hot.
How snugly the meadow pipit fits the merlin's foot.

Horseshoe

I find a rusty horseshoe where skylarks
Rise from the sheepshitty path, God-sparks,
Sound-glints for bridle and bridle hand.
I am the farrier in this townland.

Lullaby

for Eddie

The vixen will hear you cry, and the swans
On their eggless experimental nest,
And the insomniac curlew, and the leveret
That leaves a dew-path across the lawn.

Cygnus

Cygnus infuriates Achilles who just cannot kill him –
Spears bouncing off each shoulder as off a stone wall
Or cliff face, that cumbersome body blunting his sword. So,
He pummels chin and temples – knock-out punches – and
Trips him up and kneels on ribcage and adam's apple
And thrapples Cygnus's windpipe with his helmet-thongs.

But this is no triumph for Achilles: he has strangled
Neptune's son who grows webs at once between his fingers
While his hair turns snowy and feathery and his neck
Lengthens and curves out from a downy chest and his lips
Protrude as a knobbly beak through which he wheezes
And he is transformed into a – yes (hence the name) –

A white swan that flies above the bloody battlefield.

Cloudberries

You give me cloudberry jam from Lapland,
Cloudberries sweetened slowly by the cold,
Bog amber, snow-line titbits, scrumptious
And costly enough for cloudberry wars
(Diplomatic wars, my dear).
                                              Imagine us
Among the harvesters, keeping our distance
In sphagnum fields on the longest day
When dawn and dusk like frustrated lovers
Can kiss, legend has it, once a year. Ah,
Kisses at our age, cloudberry kisses.

David Harsent
The Hut In Question

Rain, midnight rain, nothing but the wild rain
On this bleak hut, and solitude, and me...
    – Edward Thomas, 'Rain'

And here it is, slap on the co-ordinates,
nothing special of course,
a tar-paper roof (is it?) nailed to sloping slats,
a door that goes flush to the floor, and grates
when you draw it back. Weather-worn, half-hidden by gorse
in full fire, it being that time of year; the window
thick with cobwebs, clarty candyfloss;
a smell of rot; things spongy underfoot.

Being here alone is easiest.
There are songbirds in the sedge
(I think it is) and a wind to clout the reeds, a test
of the place, as are these clouds: a long dark flow
pulling fast and heavy off the ridge...
Easiest given what we make of quest,
its self-regard, its fearsome lost-and-found, its need to know
the worst and wear its sorrows like a badge.

Do you get what I mean if I speak of light – half-light –
that seems to swarm: a mass
of particles folding and rolling as if you stood too close
to a screen when the image dies? The edge
of night... those forms that catch and hold
just at the brink where it's nearly but not quite.

I see, now, by that light. Rain finally coming in, the day
falling short, adrift in shades of grey,
and nowhere to get to from here, or so I guess,
with distances fading fast,
with the road I travelled by a thinning smudge,
with all that lay between us bagged and sold,
with voices in under the door that are nothing more nor less
than voices of those I loved, or said I did,
with nothing at all to mark
fear or fault, nothing to govern loss,
and limitless memory starting up in the dark.

from Broken Glass

On one side of the mirror, me, myself, in doubt.
On the other, the man I mostly want to be.
See us clear as we turn and turn about.

ℬ

I hold out my hand to the rain,
as if that 'simple act'
were something I might do again and again.

ℬ

These are the saddest snaps I've ever seen.
My father in khaki. My father in khaki. My father
in khaki. Yes. My mother in bombasine.

ℬ

Pi-dogs. A lemon sky. A Judas kiss.
A moment in some shebeen. The view you get
from behind the gun. I dreamed all this.

&

A room hanging in silence. A sunstruck window.
Doors to left and right.
A sense of decorum tells you which way to go.

&

She kicked off her shoes. She unzipped and dropped her dress,
then stalled on a vacant look.
Next night the same, and the night after that, more or less.

&

Why not grub up a smidgen of turf from his grave?
Cultivate it. Trim it as you might
toenails or hair. Soon you'll know how to grieve.

&

A teardrop mask. White gloves. Crowds in the street.
She is running a fever; she's ill.
All the more reason, she thinks, to be indiscreet.

&

The ocean at night, where something tremendous leaps.
Did I say 'sleeps'?
Who knows what the darkness discovers?

Eavan Boland
How It Was Once In Our Country

In those years I owned a blue plate,
blue from the very edges to the centre,
ocean-blue, the sort of under-wave blue
a mermaid could easily dive down into and enter.

When I looked at the plate I saw the mouth
of a harbour, an afternoon without a breath
of air, the evening clear all the way to Howth
and back, the sky a paler blue further to the south.

Consider the kind of body that enters blueness,
made out of dead-end myth and mischievous
whispers of an old, borderless
existence where the body's meaning is both more and less.

Sea-trawler, land-siren: succubus to all the dreams
land has of ocean, of its home.
She must have witnessed deaths. Of course she did.
Some say she stayed down there to escape the screams.

Seán Ó Ríordáin
My Mother's Burial

June sun in the orchard,
      the silksusurrus of afternoon,
a damn bee droning,
      ululatearing afternoon's gown.

I poured over a tarnished old letter,
      every word-sup swallowed
constricted my breath,
      every piercing word drew a tear.

I remember the very hand that wrote this,
      a hand as familiar as a face
a hand meek as an old bible,
      a hand that was a balm when sick.

And midsummer fell back into midwinter,
      the orchard became a white graveyard by the river.
In the centre of the dumb whiteness
      the black hole cried out in the snow.

Brightness of a girl on her first communion,
      brightness of the host on a Sunday altar,
brightness of the milksilk ribboning from the breast
      as they buried my mother, brightness of the sod.

My mind was demented struggling
      to grasp the funeral
when out of the white silence a robin flew down
      gently without fear, without confusion

and stayed about the grave as if aware
        of its errand, hid from everybody
except the body waiting in the coffin.
        I envied their extraordinary intimacy.

The air of paradise descended on the grave.
        The bird had a terrible saintly gaiety.
I was a man, excluded from the secret affair,
        distanced from the grave.

Sorrow's fragrance washed my wanton soul.
        Chastity's snow fell on my heart.
Now my heart is cleansed I'll bury the memory
        of the woman who carried me in her womb.

The gravediggers appeared with crude shovels
        rigorously spading clay into the grave.
I looked away, a neighbour brushing his trouser knees,
        the worldliness on the priest's face.

June sun in the orchard,
        the silksusurrus of afternoon,
a damn bee droning,
        ululatearing afternoon's gown.

I'm writing little, lame verses.
        I'd like to grab hold of the robin's tail
I'd like to scatter the spirits of those knee scrubbers.
        I'd like to make my way, sadly to the end of the day.

Translated by Greg Delanty

John Fuller
Pomme

Although the sea, with its senseless political grievance,
Has resumed its recent attempts upon the shore
And a shrapnel of spray falls back upon the rocks
In a careless sluicing, the surface is not unfriendly.
Your flip-flops in the crevice, your launching footsplash,
The squat breathing-tube, the swell of the maillot,
Reveal that you are still undaunted by the waves.
Behind the glass of your aquarium headpiece
The underseascape is a framed display,
A locked stare, as from a *dix-huitième*
Scaphandre, at an unfamiliar salon
Whose hosts are welcoming, though a trifle insolent.

Here is a slow bogue making cow-eyes, and
Suddenly changing direction like a dodgem.
Boops boops! The alarm is not absolute,
Just nature's instinct for the preferred soup.
Here are couched urchins, snugly comfortable
In the privilege of protection by Mayor Casasoprana.
Here is a mobile of squirlu nodding for the crumbs
That escape from the squelched crust in your swimming fist.
They point, not exactly in the same direction,
But in a casual variety of angles that define
The distant point that may be in their thoughts,
Like an effort in perspective by Uccello.

The mind, moving over metres like the deity
Of the water's painted ceiling, a shadow in the light,
Makes of itself what it will: a blankness lulled
By recent waking, a contented sculling over
Dreamscape; or a beneficent enquiring spirit
Noting the plutonic shelving, the mossed gabbros
And eroded diorite, like ancient unwashed dishes,
And constructing a slow history of patient collapse
On this unchanging shore. Its only witness
Is the noise of waves, the planet's primal song,
The clamour of water frustrated at a threshold,
A plea of sorts, a luxurious performance.

You hear it all the time, behind all other sounds,
Even in sleep, when it is most like the voices
Which, if you could only manage to hear them,
Are ready to expound your deepest thoughts.
Put aside your calculations then,
Coast with the swell and dip, the sudden chill
Or warmth of the currents, the sound of your own breathing.
Let this pale otherworld lead you on and on
Through colder and bluer depths to some vision
Of an absolute, the dreamwords still in the head
And hard to shake off, *comme de bien entendu.*

I will follow, as I always have done, and will do.
Of our many private performances, this is the freshest,
Our courses idly circling and meeting for a moment
In soundless acknowledgment. The sea stands for
Something that is always felt in the blood and breathing
Of our bodily lives. It is always in wait for us,
Pomme, for you are Pomme here, a little more carefree,
A bobbing, floating persona, concentrated in perception,
Full of your tenderest thoughts, Pomme, gazing out,
Graceful in water, striking from the shore,
Named by friends misreading your name in a letter,
Named in explicable error, callionymous Pomme.

And when lightning begins to describe the mountains
With its startled flicker, the clouds are affronted,
The mistral blowing, the inky sea on horseback,
And we wonder what the fishes can find to do
As the gallons roll and split upon the bay.
The shutters, though shut, stutter through the night,
The wind shaking the house like an old box,
Not quite fooled into believing that it is empty.
It makes a bid to invade our secret dreams
Where we lie prone in great drama while the clock
Faithfully records the unnoticed times
Of these encounters with an alternative past.

Whatever the outcome of these broken narratives
Of wish and betrayal in the peopled inland
Of the mind, whatever the vexing forgottenness
Of their intriguing moods and premises,
We know that in the morning all will be still.
In the morning the sea will be whispering again:
"Pomme, Pomme!" After the storm, loosened weed
Is gathered in the rocks, the slim shoals feeding,
The sun stealthy over the eastern mountains,
Pebbles sharp in the light, and always the whispers:
"Pomme, Pomme!" And down you will go to the water,
The apple of my summer life.

Omar Sabbagh
Vital

What does the palm tree say, its stalk
of tall hard ashes and concave bends,
sharkskin
caught in the dry sunshine's angles?

Rising and falling, rising and falling
in the late afternoon light, green on grey
on beige, it speaks like love or outrage,
saying, much like anything else

vital or unheard, with an urgency
before death's dark wrecking
and then the quiet that rescinds
words tall in the wind like these:

Treat me well, treat me well.
Or chip if you dare, scratch, tear, crunch,
but I will still, still with a pinpoint blare,
burst my leaves in awry hosanna –

my hair, high and light and loose, big and
sprung like a millionaire's dowry,
will ridicule all of you.
*   Upwards, the sky...*

Semyon Lipkin
Charred

and ashen I whisper,
I've been cremated.

In deserted barracks,
on Bavarian grasslands,

I think *I'm blind, confounded,*
my palate has claimed

my tongue. When Mercedes
Benz and Volkswagens

course silently, through
evening autobahns, I ask

how do I find my way
to Odessa? Born burnt,

I can't yet mourn
what it means to be alive,

or not to be alive, my cold
embers won't light a flame

Translated by Yvonne Green and Svetlana Payne

Ruth Padel
The Peaks, The Troughs

Then there was Frank
the black helicopter –
except he wasn't really a black helicopter,
they never are.

He grew up in The Just World Hypothesis
which says that people to whom bad
things happen deserve them.
Good things happen because you are good.

(When bad things happen to *you*, though,
we call that accident.)

On Sundays they took him to the Peak District
to practice levitation. All these bi-polar dreams,
he remarked, of the correspondence
theory of truth.

He stood before the Angel of the North,
catapult behind his back. His mother
combed, far as possible, his hair
over his sticking-out ears.

Gaps showed
in cover-ups of police shootings,
lies told about a war, deaths
which a Prime Minister – flightless,

like all ostriches – was responsible for,
apparently unaware
that people *have* been flying, all this time:
flying from our peaks and our troughs

into puddled cement bunkers
rustling with chains, handcuffs
and waterboards
handmade in Egypt, in Afghanistan.

In his GCSE Use of English exam
Frank wrote, "Man is the only animal
that can imagine pain."
And then – *Das Lied von der Erde*.

The Corneliu M Popescu Prize for European Poetry Translation

Since 2003, the Poetry Society and the Raitiu Charitable Family Foundation
have been running the **Corneliu M Popescu Prize** for collections of poetry
translated from a European language into English. The prize is named after
Corneliu M Popescu, a young Romanian translator killed in an earthquake in
1977. The prize is £1,000.

The Poetry Society and the Ratiu Family Foundation are happy to announce
that they will be once again accepting submissions for the Corneliu M Popescu
Prize from 17 January, 2007. The judges for this will be confirmed on the
Poetry Society website (www.poetrysociety.org.uk).

This prize, awarded every two years, is open to collections of poetry published
between May 2005 and May 2007 which feature poetry translated from
another European language into English.

The deadline for submissions is 31 May, 2007. To submit book(s) send three
copies of the publication to:
Popescu Prize, 22 Betterton Street, London, WC2H 9BX.

As I Flick Off The Remote In The Gulf I Think Of An Ancient Greek Playwright

In mem. James Wright

> *At home the same things happened.*
> *Women were widowed, then died.*
> *Parents shuffle through empty rooms*
> *Without the sons they loved.*
> *Our troops have earned this praise*
> *in our name, and we must shut up*
> *about such acts of shame.*
>   – Euripides, Trojan Women, 379-384

Euripides, with your scalpel pity and your songs,
who watched from exile in Macedonia, 403 BC,
that city where you spoke out against massacre
(blowing up the allies, for God's sake!)
sizzle in turn, the Long Walls pulled down –

you who were torn to pieces on a goat-track
by dogs – what's the use? I think of you
walking in dapply oak forests of the north
where feather-fetlocked war-stallions
are grazing meadows
which Athenian yeomen, blunting their hoes
on rockfields, would kill to cultivate.

You imagine, as you hike,
a baby-faced stranger. A god with cinnamon
sideburns, ivy sap leaking through
his microtonal *'oud,* entering every city alike:
barbarian, Greek, twin-towered, devout.

But this is March 2006. I'm on the edge of a bed
among cappucino shadows of afternoon
in the freezing cold Mövenpick Hotel. Bahrain.
100 degrees outside, and the Manager can't turn off
the air conditioning, no one can. Cement roofs roil
up and down, up and down, far as the eye
can see. Caramel domes and a salmoning sky

in the first Gulf State to find oil.
I'm watching the President of Iran
in ivory denim conduct a dance
of seven ministers on CNN.
They hop in celebration. Old men,

round and again round a desk of microphones
like the crown of stalwart hills and radio masts
about a holy city. They have enriched plutonium!
Do they feel a touch ridiculous too?
Representatives of other Arab states,
plus my friends downstairs, are all calm.

No big deal, no cause for alarm. But Washington
is talking of war. Another Abu Ghraib? Euripides,
whose microtones I lived in a long strange while:
where are your arguments now –
that frayed silk rope of human, divine,
and the same rules applying to all?

Glyn Maxwell
Flags And Candles

Flags line up an hour before they're chosen,
wave back along the row at others like them.
Candles sit in boxes or lie still,

sealed, and each imagines what will happen.
Flags will not accept the explanation
of why they were not needed as they are now.

Candles feel they're made of stuff that's soft
for a good cause, though maybe not their own cause.
Tall flags love all flags if it's these flags.

Small flags are okay about immense flags.
Candles doze in xylophones of colour,
thrilled their purpose may be merely pattern.

Flags are picked out one by one. The others
group around the gap and say Gap, what gap?
Candles dream of something that will change them,

that is the making of and death of candles.
Flags don't dream of anything but more flags.
The wind is blowing; only the landscape changes.

Candles have the ghost of an idea
exactly what the wick is for: they hope so.
Flags are hearing that you can't see flags

at night, not even giants in a windstorm.
Candles have read that they can cry all day
and go unnoticed even by old candles.

When I wave flags, flags think it's the world waving
while flags are holding fast. When I light candles,
the sense of something reverently bowing

holds me and I tremble like the shadows.
Flags again know nothing and they're flying.
Candles shed a light and burn to darkness.

℘

Kaspar Hauser

My dream of her
was memories in heaps and the whole morning
at her age now

I think of her
is memories in heaps. In the great daylight
I do nothing

but see stars
like the wolf-boy they sat down in a world
of nonsense.

E.A. Markham
The Story Of A Revolution

Grandmother is reading Ruskin's *Seven Lamps of Architecture*.
The year is 1956 in Coderington, St. Caesare
And the Revolution is forty years off, so scholars argue
Over how much reading grandmother has got through in the years
Since she died, a detail well worth mention, as when it comes
The Revolution will be disguised as natural phenomena
And presented as hurricane and volcano; and the name Krueger,
Appearing in the records of the time, will be an error.

So grandmother, alive and reading her book, can be allowed
To be distracted a little by whispers about Krueger.
Pewter, the boy, destined for England, sixteen years old let's say,
Buys a sugar-cake at Krueger's shop: there's no such shop, of course.
When he describes it, it's Mr. Lee's shop. What, grandmother asks,
Has Krueger done with Mr. Lee? Nobody knows: then why
Aren't they curious? Nellie, the maid, is reading those servants' parts
In Molière that make you hopeful. Pewter is reading Hakluyt.

There's little thought now of the revolution that didn't happen.
Though Krueger makes an appearance out of context, as a comic;
And Miss Na and Tan Tan and Uncle Mike are given more credit
For having lived in those times. And the boy, Pewter, tells the story
Of early days in England unable to talk to workmates
About Hakluyt, because either Hakluyt or Pewter's accent
Was unfamiliar. So here's Krueger in costume, gun in hand.
I am Krueger, he says. No discussion. No nonsense. Chop chop.

Alan Brownjohn
Ludbrooke

His Compliment

A friend says, 'Ludbrooke, you're a conniving sod.'
No smile, no approval or disapproval,
Statement of fact. And he reflects on it
In one of his usual venues of reflection:
The bath, the Co-op check-out queue, in bed
Before he gets up. Yes, he's felt exactly that
For many decades. He knows his instinct for finding
A devious route to any given objective
Other men would approach by motorway,
Breaking down en route. Among the smoking wrecks
Of all their projects he moves with ruthless care
And predatory compassion, grinding small.
Ludbrooke pretends he never grinds at all.

His Chivalry

He stops at his local zebra, in front
Of a girl braking her Ford for him radiantly
Visible through her screen of untinted glass.
She has stopped for Ludbrooke alone, he feels favoured
For the first time in weeks, doesn't falter at the kerb,
Strides out with his head turned smilingly towards her,
Puts a kiss on the forefinger and middle finger
Of his right hand, for once an unprepared impulse,
And wafts it to her – and she's smiling back.
A good day, he concludes, as he pushes through
The doors of a supermarket he's ashamed to enter,
And strolls down aisles of plastic groceries thinking
I can use that kiss again, I really can.

His Pride

He is not prepared to stand around waiting
For someone to attach the ribbon of the Order
Of the Spare Prick to his soup-stained lapel.
He likes to be noticed, to be the arresting
Centre of an attention he disclaims.
He must never be left alone, and if ignored
When being sociable, he will leave the room
Hoping people will have noticed and say, Well, Ludbrooke
Left pretty early – I wonder why? He knows absence can be
More imposing then presence if done properly.
Tonight he has been somewhere just to remind
The buggers that he still exists. Back home early,
In house arrest, he opens the spare bottle.

His Red

He believes, at around the eleventh glass
– But really, it's just been one continuous glass
Replenished before it's ever emptied,
And that ends the second bottle, *nessa par?* –
He has crossed the boundary from creative
Optimism to embark upon achievement.
He toasts *Achievement!* Possibilities
Come on display now like the endless wares
Of an Istanbul carpet salesman filling up
His tiny cup with coffee, brilliances unrolling
Long vistas ahead of him, happy paths
– That end in colourless nowheres. So... the third cork...
And the twelfth glass. Lifted to *Relaxed despair.*

His Physique

Ludbrooke is tall but cannot wish he was
The moderate size of Ridyard, a smaller man
Who seems to attract simultaneous pity and desire
From tall strong girls. He suspects that man with his latest.
She takes a small-scale sort of feminine beauty
Past the point where he can describe it, and on
To the verge of perfection. It's any movement she makes...
She has only to turn towards him with her ambivalent
Half-smile for him to gaze down, he imagines,
As at a locket painted for someone to carry
To some Peninsular War or other and maintain
His loyalty; never tested, then, by what buzzes
In her handbag now. That's *Ridyard*'s ringtone...

John Fuller
The Dance

World-eager, the joint
Straightened to a point
(Solomon rose in stone)
And to the temple
Came the temptress
(O my dove, my columb).

Shoulders stretched
And nails far-fetched
(Solomon rose in robes)
She asked again
What will remain
(O my dove, my quotient).

Though night advances
Shall we dance?
(Solomon rose in wine)
And still she asked
All that had passed
(O my dove, my trouble).

Ankle turned out
Lets toes sprout
(Solomon rose in blood)
Arms flung wide
At elbows divide
(O my dove, my double).

Knuckles unwhiten
As hands untighten
(Solomon rose in bone)
Part in a fan,
Stretch to their span
(O my dove, my nature).

Neck unlocks
And the heart knocks
(Solomon rose in fire)
And the waist twists
And turning wrists
(O my dove, my fixture).

Nothing that she required
Appeared to tire him
(Solomon rose again)
The night was entire
In its dome of fire
(O my dove, my turtle).

World-full, the heart
Must play its part
(Solomon rose again)
Dancing the answers
Dancing the dance
(O my dove, O my dove).

Krystyna Milobędzka

***

how to make a star
brighter touched, darker said
before there it is is
is is not

to laugh out, shrug your shoulders
spread your arms just so

Translated by Elżbieta Wójcik-Leese

David Morley
The Charges On Midsummer Night For
The Coventry Mysteries

Adapted from records of early English Drama

o p*ai*d for a pece of tymber for ye Axeltre, & for Nayles for it,
   ye Pagent whereof halfe is to spare in William Catesby's house
o Item payd for Sope for all ye wheeles
o Item payd for 3 Worlds
o Item payd for payntyng Hell Mouth and me*n*dying hyt
o Item payd for openyng and shuttyng the Dores and kypyng the Wynd

o Item payd for settyng the Worlds on ffyer & blacking ye Sowles facys
o Item payd to the 3 damnyd Sowles & 3 Saved Sowles
o Item payd thus to 2 Demens
o Item payd the 2 wormes of Consyens
o Item paid to Death

o Item payd to the Mother of Death
o Item payd ffor a peyre of gloves ffor God
o Payd up also for the gybbyt of Jei3e
o Item payd to Mr Fawston for hangyng Judas
o Item paide to Mr Fawston for his Coc-crowyng

o Item payd for 3 Angells
o Item paide ffor wasshyng the Angells surplisses
o Item payd to losephe
o Item payd to God
o And also paide to the Spirite of God

o Item payd to Jesus
o Item payd to Mary
o Item payd to Pylate
o Item to the litell dying Chyld
o Item payd for this Poem

Yang Lian
Home

for Yoyo

1.

The cat who ought to be here strolls between the furniture,
supplying a blank to the rainy day.   Bottles are being washed –
organs hanging shining outside the body.
Each has a ringing pair of north and south poles
binding ice and snow with absent lines of magnetic force.
Another hour moves you and me into
the space-craft   holding hands   screaming   eyes closed.
Imagine being secured in the mad star-sky.

2.

Your thin shining snores   circle far away.
Night has a delicately-carved cut-off comet's tail,
this house floats on water, following
the form of water   continually darkening against the phosphorescence,
sweeping the world away with the second-hand's tongue.

A poet needs a cave   no smaller than
his intolerable stupidity,   the walls change and change again
and a painting hung on the emptiness   makes itself at home in the
     world.
The sound of music is put into the old book of the past:
a lovely *miniature,*   it must be a *miniature* to move toward the
     art of the pen.
The lamp takes over a moth's self,
the speed of light wakes violently in flesh
enjoying an azure dinner, catching up with the horizon,
still smelling the fragrance of the paint: to rip off skin means to rip off
you and me   and the next made-to-measure morning.

Greg Delanty
The Naming Of Clouds

To Katharine Washburn, 1943-2000

This is the weather you loved most of all,
        a snugness of charcoal cloud with rainfall.
Altostratus I thought at first, not opacus nebulosus.
        But now I'm sure the cloud
            is nimbostratus,
        it being both a close shroud
            and halo
            on the inscape outside my window.
For anyone today passing through here
        for the first time, they'll not know
            the Adirondacks were laid out over there,
        having vanished in the nimbus air
across the stratus of the lake, just as anyone who
        didn't know you will hardly realize you were here.
Or why we peer through the cloud to wherever you
        have gone, shrouded in nimbostratus Katharinus.

Jackie Kay
Darling

You might forget the exact sound of her voice,
Or how her face looked when sleeping.
You might forget the sound of her quiet weeping
Curled into the shape of a half moon,

When smaller than her self, she seemed already to be leaving
Before she left, when the blossom was on the trees
And the sun was out, and all seemed good in the world.
I held her hand and sang a song from when I was a girl –

Heil Ya Ho Boys, Let her go Boys
And when I stopped singing she had slipped away,
Already a slip of a girl again, skipping off,
Her heart light, her face almost smiling.

And what I didn't know, or couldn't see then,
Was that she hadn't really gone.
The dead don't go till you do, loved ones.
The dead are still here holding our hands.

Alan Jenkins
At The Grave Of Joseph Brodsky

1.

You made your last trip in the Jumbo's freezing hold
(you were, or so they told me, sealed in zinc).
You would not have minded in the least – cold
was your element, it helped you to think,
and so Stockholm was where you did your work
while sweat and paranoia hissed off the street
in Brooklyn, where you punished your old Merc.
Joseph, how you would have suffered from the heat
the day we buried you in Venice. Two days before
the city had been watercolour, or gouache
behind its heat-haze; now I looked back at the shore
as the vaporetto rocked at marble steps, awash –
salt sea and women's tears contending there –
and walls and trees evaporated, turned to wobbly air.

2.

I thought of how, in fifty years or so, all this,
this miracle of wood and stone and light and water
will have gone to myth and water, like Atlantis...
Kneeling at your graveside, your wife and daughter
made a *Pietà*. A priest offered prayers and thanks
for you, one part grief to two parts uplift.
The (mainly Jewish) audience of Russians, Yanks
and Poles caught no more than the general drift.
It didn't matter, not one bit. What mattered
was that you were gone for good and we were left.
I saw you order dim sum and pull out a tattered
sheaf of poems from your jacket-pocket, Joseph,
I heard you haggle over adverbs like a street-trader in
a market in some Middle-European town. You'd always win...

3.

And now you lay alone and cold and in the ground.
And where you lay, you shared the cypress-cool and loam
not with headstones in Cyrillic, but Jew-hating Pound –
just the place to make your final home...
Home! Half your life in exile as a resident
alien made you at home in any borrowed flat.
Now this absurd wreath with its ribbon, *From the President* –
of Russia! As if you'd have wanted that –
a last, grotesque, half-desperate lunge
at claiming back their once-unwanted son –
as if a wreath could make amends for, could expunge
two parents' deaths, all that was said and done...
The beauty next to me was sobbing (I cried too),
a tendril twined on a cypress-trunk for love of you...

4.

But all knew just what we had loved, and lost.
What didn't kill you made you stronger. Verse
climbed free of petty cruelties and *poshlost.*
I could almost hear you say, *Don't spare the hearse,*
yah? I disappeared, as it were, in the dead of winter.
(Great shade, forgive me. But I'd like to think that Wystan
might have penned an elegy on me as well –
the greater on the lesser.) It was cold as hell –
as Archangel. If you'd jammed mercury in my sphincter
it would have registered, to say the least, zero;
as it would on Alias Island, outside, in the cistern,
far away among the wooden and the white facades
of Stockholm, and even in my study. Into which comes –
bored with his usual haul of junkies, buskers, bums –

5.

a familiar stranger, fingering my soul.
Did I go quietly? Of course. To play the hero
is not really to my taste, yah? Not, in fact, my role.
Besides, it wasn't some small-town Napoleon or Nero
they'd sent to get me, not some commissar,
some strutting medi-ogre trying to prise my lid,
not some Freudian critic poking in my Id
and not some drunken émigré in a Greenwich Village bar,
groaning in my face; nor the surgeon with his knife
seeking entrée to my entrails. Not some hack looking for the Life
of the poet outside of his (alas, so lengthy) work.
It was neither saint nor sinner, journalist nor jerk
nor even my ex-jailer with a full deck of cards
but – Horace-Hardy-Frost – the voice was a bard's

6.

that addressed to me, in the friendliest terms,
the news that my time had come to feed some worms,
that I wasn't going to croak 'in some big hotel
to the consternation of the personnel'
like Wystan, but right here, from cardiac arrest, translator
of last persons to the absent tense, the lesser to the greater.
But as I told you in that bird-and-bard-filled garden
in Way-on-Hye, language doesn't have to beg time's pardon,
language cannot be defeated, no matter what –
the organized cruelty of the state, the infinite, red-hot
vulgarity of the human heart – and it's good to those
by whom it lives, despite biography's plain prose,
our lah-di-dah lives. It won't be silenced by neglect or fame
or any nihilistic garbage. Now I've left my mortal frame

7.

I am what I left in verse. I miss my wife and daughter,
miss everyone I loved. That's tough. But solitude
goes with the métier; the plane of regard, no longer skewed
by desire, is fixed on the loveliness of Earth
and my esteemed self, one part flesh to five of water,
scents wet seaweed, happiness, home. Beware these cissies'
times, when people kill for kicks. Kisses, kisses.
The sun throbbed down. Your daughter ran and played
and chased a butterfly in and out of cypress-shade.
What did she care for mysteries of death and birth?
How soon would she begin to understand
that to die is just this: cowardly or brave,
to lie at last far from the touch of any hand
while others look on, helpless, round a grave?

Shi Tao
from Dedicated To The Book Of The Dead

8-11 August 2004, Taiyuan

I.

I forget all
language starts
from the simplest words.

Memory like a lamp
in the slave's hand:
kneeling, I beg it to last.

Night moves on inch
by inch. Before dawn's first
light I search for a life.

No news of a boat
mooring alongside.
Over my face

a sea-breeze plays –
its taste is called
sorrow.

IV.

All my life I'm confused
by the same bearings:
sand-storm, then curtain up –

I dread looking West,
Purgatory's ultra-violet
testing my middle years.

V.

Fat strawberry heads
filled with cloud dreams, the male's
Dali dream-world.

Egypt's Book of The Dead –
those faces on the page,
their skin still gives off heat.

With my stick
of a finger, I trace
my own frozen features.

Everywhere, the foes
of the dying intone their
chant: 'Song of the world'.

Translated by John Weston

Amanda Aizpuriete
That Probably Would Be Best

English version

That probably would be best – not to care
about printshops, not to allow access to my words to those solemn
and symmetrical letters – to leave it all in the curves of my
handwriting, jerky and uneven like life.
It would be best to take the pages covered with writing and fold them
into ships, birds, and butterflies, then throw them up in the air, into
the wind, fire, water.
Later they will reverently touch the earth
in the form of ashes or wet scraps of paper, or tired
butterflies. The earth
will sprout a flower with four crescent shaped petals – my most
beautiful quatrain. Pollen, caught in the wind, will fly searching for
new soil, people will inhale the strangely fragrant air... And in a
different life,
a poem turned lover will embrace me, a poem I will have long
since forgotten,

Dat Wid Laekly Be Best

Sheltlandic version

Dat wid laekly be best – no ta budder
aboot printshops, nor hae mi wirds gleg
i da grip o a kirsen keyboard – ta leave hit aa i da curvin whenks o mi
ain hand, da reffels, da cuggliness lik life.
Hit wid be best ta tak mi pages smoored wi wirds an fowld dem
inta boats, birds an butterflees, dan baal dem up i da air, inta
wind, fire, watter.
Eftir a while, peerie-wyes, dey'll sain da aert
as ess or as a flaachter o sabbin smatters, or ootmaggit
butterflees. Da aert
'll sprout a flooer wi fowr petals, shapit lik new möns, mi
boanniest fowr-lined verse. Pollen, ta'en wi da wind, 'll flee seekin
new möld, fock 'll breathe in a fine, uncan niff... an in a
different life,
da beloved wan dat wis mi poem, 'll hadd me i da bosie, a poem A'm
already foryatten,

Translated by Christine De Luca in discussion with the Latvian author

Marie Étienne
from Some Of Them Are Japanese

l. In the autumn, they fly off.
They reach the equator, they venture so far that they
have nothing to eat.
They come back so soon that they are cold and
they die.
That they are hungry and they die.
They die twice, ten times.
Some of them are sedentary and some are migrants.
Their short wings are bad for flying.
Some of them are Japanese.
They fly two miles, five miles, ten miles. Without
landing.
What are they looking for? We look for it.
Their way is the way of the glaciers.
At the moment of departure, the air is troubled, but empty.
Even in cages, they keep moving.

3. All of them aren't in the air.
Not obliged to be.
Some of them dig holes, some swim, some climb.
Never leave their trees, or only for grooming.
Which goes on, and on.
Were usually massacred.
Once they were abundant.
Darkened the sky.
But the storm came from below, despite what was believed.
The storm exterminated them, sold wholesale on the marketplace,
dead skin, useless meat.
Threw them to the pigs, used them for fertilizer.
What were they called again?
Birds of paradise?

4.They have the gift of song provided that they learn.
Singing is learned like anything else.
Like walking to the end of the world.
Lifting up one's eyes.
Offering one's hands.
Sitting down in front of the door, head bent.
Out the open window, looking at what burns, what
is beyond the trees, the shadow that comes with the evening.
Leaving.
Go on, go on!
They have memory.
For example, when the door is too large, when a dream
worries them, when the sun rises and sets, they understand
their happiness.
They stay, they are not afraid.
Less grey than usual.

5. During the massacres, some of them were spared.
They didn't have enough gold on their necks.
Later, when they sang, when they spoke in the words of their former
leaders, of their slaughtered leaders, no one understood them.
Their language too had been exterminated.
Which proves that even the best singing does not suffice
to hold your territory, your female.
It's also necessary to fly at night.
Never to return, even years later, to a dangerous spot.
To continue otherwise and elsewhere.
To be a better singer, a better fighter.
To create constant variations.
To walk amidst changing colors, around the miraculous circle.
To mark the earth.
To draw a square with one's own number.

10. The child has taken the words, the birds, the winds.
He has divided them into a hundred sections.
I put in every part of my life. I love that.
To kiss the night, its edges, that's my kitchen.
He drinks darkness in gulps; he sees clarities.
As they say, the other world.
Black rains down, strong-brewed white.
Peelings and feathers.
Shadows sometimes, and temptations.
Damp blows behind the windowpane.
Shadow-rings in daylight.
Behind the closed shutters, outdoor light.
The colorless colors, soon washed-out, of the desert, where the
child walks among white rocks.
King of a hundred horsemen.

Translated by Marilyn Hacker

Alison Brackenbury
On A February Night

When I dream of my mother, she is a voice.
Which is, I suppose, how we first know our mothers
In those forgotten waters. Women often talk too much.
Watch those who are quiet; they may be the ones
Who break a life, then smile. I am still whole.
But as I hear my mother, in the dream's dull room
Something slips then flutters, liquid as her lilt,
Tilts level with the air. It is a bat.
"Look, look," I say, but dreaming, no-one sees.

Bats slept in the tall house, the one she loved,
In sash cords' gaps. My sister hated them.
My father drove them out. Look how they rise,
In clouds of voices, leaf for winter trees.

Julia Casterton
Goblins

It can take eons to get rid of them.
You lie half-conscious in a hospital bed.
Strong hands fill you up with glucose, blood and iron.
Yet the memory of goblins sucking out your womb,

your bone marrow,
won't leave you. By day you doze,
at night you fight them in your body,
a *lucha continua*.

Your vision fades, sense fails, you float
on the chance their antics in last night's parade
signal that they are bored, and might move on
to another foolish eater, suicide, or sister.

Sean Borodale
Lyrigraph For A Lady Chatting
(From Reading To Bath By Train)

She puts her tickets in a row.
Says, 'I've that one and that...
have you ever seen anything so ridiculous,
all for one journey.'

Here's the inspector. Enters an aisle of duty.
Takes a ticket [*A whole field of mustard's going past*]
'They're not tickets, they're reservation cards,' she says.

A fantastic laughing lady, putting her tickets away
[*Under a cloud, along a county*]
'I meant to ask Monique what that lemon souffle was.
It was light, it was very nice,' she says.

[*A station's platforms like two greyhounds pass*]

She lowers her mouth [*To talk of her mother*]
'I've still got that fear. She always goes for the fish,
so I take my cue. Fish it shall be.'

Her smile's recess, the mouth inside itself,
is black as a cave for melancholia
[*She fills with laughs, just as the sea fills caves*]

She enters a relapse of non-laughter, gently says,
'And if I always did the same for you, you'd be as good.
He was right to leave as he did, but not to die
before she'd let him go... he died a long time back,
fourteen years I think.' [*All buried in her head*]

This delicate minute by minute fast old age.

Her laughing's hardened like a stalk, saying,
'Wants to go to summer ball, all this nonsense.'
Her face is two cheeks fallen in two,
once were wings for words, for breath to fly,
saying [*Of her mother*] 'When he goes to the States
she feels she doesn't know where he is.'

[*A ring on her finger private as a room behind a door*]

'I left a meal for Mum, she's ninety-two
[*Whilst in a thought, whilst two brown eyes*]
and went to collect him from the airport.
My car's battered but it goes like a bomb and I love it.
'They are the best ones,' says her friend.
'Keep it till it dies,' [*Passing roads between factories
passing kings in cars*] she says.

[*With nothing else above, nothing else but the weather*]

'Do you have a sunshine roof?' 'Oh, yes.'
[*With teeth drawn in towards the tongue which croaks*]
'It's only because it's so old, I feel I have to change it.'
And says, 'I'm always conscious of the need for friendship,
I'm very cautious, I mean, my mother said,
don't ever leave. I'm sixty-eight,' she says.
[*With nothing, nothing else but the sky of the length of her life above*]

CENTREFOLD

The ghost of a third melody between left hand and right in Chopin and Schubert – I would love my lines to reverberate like that.
—Michael Longley

Before, Behind, Between, Above, Below:

The Poem That Was A Play That Was A Novel.

GLYN MAXWELL

You're beautiful but crying.

Aren't you? Beautiful but crying.

Just sittin here, beautiful but crying.
I'm sorry I don't understand what you're saying, I keep thinking you mean someone else.

[from *The Girl Who Was Going To Die*]

I've just finished writing a novel that starts like that. The central character, the eponymous Girl, speaks in roman font; everyone else speaks in italics. The authorial presence consists – obviously – in what they say, who says it, when and to what end, but there's no narrator, no other viewpoint, no third person, no first, no second. There's a fourth wall, of course, which there isn't.

This isn't an original idea, but I didn't steal it in the market, I had it in my house, so it's my idea. It's a very hazardous way to write, it's a bit uncommon, but I would be certifiably insane if I didn't at least believe that years of writing theatre had equipped me to write distinguishable voices without hopping around behind them murmuring 'I said', 'he murmured', 'she smiled', 'we wondered' – or indeed, as in the never-quite-satisfying publications of play-texts, holding big signs up in the margin with people's names on them. Who in the room is doing that? Who in our lives is doing that?

MAXWELL: No one.

So theatre might equip one to write, so to speak, framelessly, but *The Girl Who Was Going To Die* is not theatre. It's a novel resembling theatre. Halfway through the writing of it, I realized that the book would complete a perverse set of three, because I've also written plays resembling poems, and lately a book of poems resembling a novel. Consider the wagons circled. But none of them is any of them, and it occurred to me that examining the ways that none of them is any of them might be more interesting than simply assenting to the plausible diagnoses: that I am pathologically incapable of writing in received forms, or, as has been kindly said – as by an expert of a problem child – that I am 'restless'.

I'd not consciously chosen to explore the dimensions between genres with such geometric fullness, but I've found myself there in three well-nigh deserted counties, and since from that vantage one can see clearly the crowded skylines of the cities of British poetry, fiction, and theatre at far points on the horizon, I've reached the conclusion that the borders between them all are porous, negotiable, fascinating places, sites of smuggling, bartering and intermarriage. So, in the spirit of those graceful little essays Eliot wrote about his experiences in theatre – craft-based, anecdotal, and specifically addressed to writers in the future who might find them helpful – I thought I'd try and write up my findings.

A Novel That's Not A Play

What made me think it was worth trying to write a book entirely in monologue, dialogue or choruses was the following phrase:

What's that, a margarita?

I felt that if I saw that written down I would assume the following things: that there are two people (it's all we need or want at first), that the two people know each other (it's rude to a stranger), but not that well (one friend would know what another friend liked to drink), and that they are in a bar (if they were in the house of the margarita-drinker such a complex concoction would have been mentioned by now). That they're female (that one may just be me), that the speaking friend has only just arrived on the scene (one notices a big drink in front of someone), that the speaker is thinking she might like that drink too (people try out foreign words for flavour), and that she likes a drink more than she wants to say (she knows what a margarita looks like but she still asks.)

These deductions are not watertight, but they're reasonably shipshape. One speculates into the middle-distance: that it's evening, that the speaker has come from work, that her work is stressful because a drink is the first thing she's thinking of, that it's crowded. That they're not poor, that they're not in the countryside, that they're not old, that it's not long ago. We would think of the times we might be in or near a situation in which *What's that, a margarita?* gets said.

On top of that pictures might come: that she's taking off her coat when she says it, that they're at a bar not a table, that it's crowded, that young men in suits are everywhere. Or not those things but similar things. This is the region where each reader diverges into the images that relate to his or her own mental hinterland. That's fine. A writer who thinks he can control that country really is out of his mind. And whatever, nail it in the next line. Nail it in the line before. The point is the set doesn't matter. Or it matters, but not much. It's background. The physical senses can't focus on both fore- and background. What matters is what voices say, how they say, why they say.

A conventional prose narrative imagines environment and tries to describe it. What the isolation of dialogue does is to suggest environment in only the tone and matter of the voice. In that way it resembles bare-stage or impressionistic theatre, as opposed to the pseudo-realism of sets, costumes, props and so on. It reminds us that much of prose fiction is just stage-direction or, these days, screenplay. Shaw's stage-directions are the length of short stories. Some published play-texts can't even shut up about silence: they say "*(Beat.)*" as if we required the author to intervene, tom-tom at the ready, right on cue. You mean space: make space.

The Girl Who Was Going To Die may resemble theatre, then, but it's not it. It's meant to be experienced as words on a page. It matters when the page turns, it matters what can be glimpsed on the recto while one is reading the verso, it matters what springs the surprise of being on the next verso, hidden from the last recto. It matters when a page is blank. Which is as old as *Tristram Shandy* but heigh-ho.

In the heightened language of great theatre, a broad spectrum of sensory experience is compressed into lines of an articulate profundity that is not in itself realistic: "But, soft! What light at yonder window breaks?" These words are meant to fill an actual space with – in this case – darkness, chilliness, dawn, desire, anticipation. Isolated dialogue in a novel has to act that way on the mind without prompting from an authoritative – or authorial – voice. Late great Henry Green comes close to that effect, but a good radio play is closer: it's a reduction of sensory resources to a single instrument, and then playing that instrument for all it's worth.

I've heard it said that the BBC's first ever broadcast radio play took place in a mineshaft, where trapped miners spoke in pitch darkness. There's an auroral beauty to that, the caution of a bright but very literal child thinking things through: we can't see who's speaking, so we... can't see who's speaking. The story may be apocryphal, but it's too late to unhear it. I wanted to include in the characterization of my voices an element of their very loneliness *on the page*, their 'flatness', their life in two dimensions; that what they say or is said to them constitutes the only human warmth; everything else is silence, or time passing, or minds changing, or just the background, the great panoply around us *at which we are not looking right now*. And what we think is bringing us closer in our new-look lives seems to me like something else, because our world is full of people saying into little shiny gadgets *Where are you? Where are you now? I'm on the train!* and what percentage of your relationship with your friends involves actually looking at them? Or even hearing their voices? Don't most of your acquaintances communicate in the same font?

All writers are accustomed to that giddy feeling of having created people, when it blurs into something else – maybe around the margarita hour – and one wonders what they think of you, but it's not just a foray into fantasy, it's an effect of working in a certain form, like paint-fumes or pulled muscles.

Beckett is only the latest – though among the greatest – to drive to its end the logic of a form: theatre as a world where only the sound one makes is proof-of-life. (Anyone like me who finds Beckett's theatre colder than reality should probably postpone that verdict till very late in the day.)

There is no appeal, no soothing of perspective, no mediation, in a story without a teller. Narrative is always consoling. It can be a thousand things, but it's always consoling *as well*. Third-person is consoling in an obvious way, for we are in the presence of *one who made it*, that is, both created it and survived it – but first-person is consoling too: "I sat in a bar with my margarita as the murderer walked in" – well okay, but you're here now, you're fine – and present-tense too: "I sit in a bar with my margarita as the murderer walks in" – no you don't, you sit at a desk and say you do. Wanna take a break?

Characters without narrators have a life different from their chaperoned cousins. They are saying – or the one I made is saying – I'm not a character in a book, I am real, so the only person who is trying to make me a character in a book, trying to subject me to the discolorations of plot, structure, surprise and excitement, is you. You in the extra dimension. You up there, if you're there. Maybe you're not there.

Plays That Are Not Poems

All the plays I've had published, and all the plays I've had staged, have resembled poetry, in the sense that they've been written in lines of verse. But they are not poems, or poetry, or anything much like it. The journey has not so much been one of learning but unlearning. That's what Eliot said his journey was like.

Because, in English, the plays we prize the highest were written by poets, a contemporary poet is bound to arrive in the world of theatre believing that what theatre lacks is what he possesses – lyric intelligence, mystery, beauty – whereas in fact he can be of use in theatre only by jettisoning all of them. The most valuable discussions I have with directors are when they say of some line 'I don't get this' and I start explaining how lovely or witty or true it is. As soon as I hear myself doing that, we both know that whatever it is it's going in the bin. The director lets me rattle on a bit, how interesting, but the canary has expired, the air is bad. Use it in a poem, the director says, forgetting it.

What poets actually can smuggle through the stage-door is what they know about form and what they know about silence. A writer who works in stanzaic form knows something about structure, knows something about the relation between freedom and constriction, or the dizzying gulf between sound and no-sound, that the free-verse writer – and many writers who confine themselves to prose – may not know. That the white space at the end of the line is the mist we walk into every moment of our lives. To end a line is to be unaware of quite what is coming next, to *half-know*; to feel the lungs and throat and lips readying themselves, *but for what, for this? yes for this...* Verse animates that unawareness of the moment to come: that we are ready to shape it, sketch it out ahead – we know the rhythm it has but that's all we know... Prose has a tendency to finesse this, gloss it with more of itself. Great prose is prose where you don't notice.

For what's a verse line other than a metaphor for a facet of mortality? Pentameter as breath is merely an example of it, though obviously by leagues the most successful. Why is the violin the star of the orchestra? Because the movement of the bow resembles an exhalation, in length and sweetness and energy waning, and the effort that will be required to go on: "I can't go on. I'll go on." All the enduring instruments resemble something in the body. How can one explain the power of a great rock song other than to feel how it electrifies all points of the body's compass? The lyrics as the mind, the guitar as the hands, the drums as the heartbeat, the bass as, well, whatever else looms large. Such excitement makes us all into that troll-like homunculus you see in diagrams, where our proportions are dictated by where we feel most intensely.

But all enduring verse has got the breath right, whether it's the serene undulation of repose, the gasp or sigh of emotional disruption, or the air parcelled out by walking. The trimeters and tetrameters and rhymes of lyric don't have a walking-gait but the glad balance and sway of a song played at a bright standstill: "Fear no more the heat o'the sun / Nor the furious winter's rages...", "Go, lovely Rose – / Tell her that wastes her time and me, / That now she knows...", "Busy old fool, unruly Sun, / Why dost thou thus, / Through windows, and through curtains / call on us?" Sonnet length is roughly the amount of time one can articulate love or loss of it before the emotion itself draws one back out to life, so its conclusion has to be ringing, must propel one from thought. Too much said or too little is unconvincing in the realm of love. Terza rima is a way of capturing thought-waves in passing time and passing space, with rhymes playing the role of thoughts rising and fading: *origin, development, echo*... Mandelstam says that the very essence of Dante is *tread*: "How many pairs of sandals did Alighieri wear out on the goat-paths of Italy?"

Verse is the voice that sails on breath. This makes the verse line nothing less than the distillation of how it feels to be living. In which situation not everything is a poem, not everything circles or dances towards a chime of awareness, not everything is shocking or exciting or even true. Not everything is said by one person into silence. Not everything ends with the salute of the rhymer, the sigh of the romantic, the wink of the intellectual or the empty gesture of the wised-out postmodern. Most things end with someone else saying something back, someone who doesn't want to hear silence either, doesn't want to hear the world turning. All this is a description not of poems, and not of fiction, but of verse theatre, or, as I call it, theatre.

Prose in theatre, like free-verse – by which I mean verse employing no poetic measures of any kind – will always tend to foreground an author's intellect and accord it a freedom to create or control that no respiring consciousness actually possesses. If you cannot hear breath you're where, you're in a library, I mean a library *these days*. And before I am entombed under a barrage of names of great prose dramatists – the single word "Chekhov" would do it – I go back to what I said about Beckett, driving the logic of the form to its end.

Characters in Chekhov seem to me almost *singing* upon silence, upon their anxiety to stay warm, to be heard, to be considered, brought into spotlight: "My love is like a stone tied round my neck; it's dragging me down to the bottom; but I love my stone!" What we love in the stage-characters we love is related to their desire to remain in the light, so we love the talkers, the liars, the boasters and self-dramatizers – the soft spot we have for them is a beam of light. A great contemporary poet said the difficulty with writing theatre was getting people on and off the stage, and that cuts to the heart of the matter. Nobody wants to leave. For the form *itself* is a brightness, the action is a light in the forest, it's where we are, and we love and judge and remember the faces at our campfire.

And poets ought to do more of this work because poets are writers whose age-old forms exist to make sound unforgettable, and to make sound unforgettable is to purify silence, to make the fire crackle in the forest.

Poems That Are Not A Novel

Finally, *The Sugar Mile* is a book of poems that tells a story. Only a fool would say it's a novel, but one has, so there we go. As with the book I call a novel, which I discussed above, it matters when the pages turn. Space is important. There are blank pages and crossings-out and some things are almost too faint to read. It's in order.

But it's a book of poems. I remember picking up from Practical Criticism long ago the idea that every poem stood alone, unaffected, unmediated by knowledge, biography, history. I never trusted that idea because I didn't think it related to anything in experience, and for me that's always a hole beneath the waterline. I wanted a book of poems where the air really trembled between the pieces: a boy says this loudly because a girl said something softly. She sings a lullaby because he just swore. Forms tighten and loosen as the clock ticks. A man goes quieter when he drinks, then louder when he drinks again. The agglomeration of everything moves what's next. In the spaces between these poems sometimes the world is on fire. Sometimes someone is waking up, sometimes it's just pages turning. When Sony, sooner than you think, brings out the literary equivalent of the iPod, it is rumoured that you will be able to hear the "pages" "turning". Which is "nice".

So. In all three of these forms, novel-as-dialogue, verse theatre, and poems-as-story, I suppose I've been searching for an authenticity that isn't realism, trying to find it in the very fibre of the form. Voices on a page are lonely, troubled by the sky, by a sense of authority dwelling just beyond sight; voices on a stage are looking for the warmth of spotlight, the brief candle, they want to be lit while they live.

In *The Sugar Mile* the characters speak in poems, they hold the floor for a moment, they sing accompanied. I used quite regular, traditional forms – quatrains, sestinas, couplets, a lot of rhyme – because I wanted the effect of photographs in old silver and copper frames, artifacts preserved, the dead remembered as they were at their best. I tried to match forms with ages: repetitive couplets for an old man, passionate lyrics for a girl with her fingers crossed, solid quatrains for a patriotic lad, rough prose for a liar: Old England singing the sound of its past as it faces extinction, huddled in a book.

I-as-myself am the only character who gets interrupted, by an old man on page two, which is obviously the tolling of the Mariner, but I was also thinking of Chaucer, my first hero of narrative playfulness, who made the Canterbury tale told by "Geoffrey Chaucer" so boring his own Pilgrims told him to shut up: "thy drasty rymyng is nat worth a toord." That was daybreak on a long journey for me, and if there's one thing these forays into forms-between-forms undeniably have in common, it is that in all three cases I myself, as myself, say nothing. Which is maybe why I've turned up now, now everyone's gone and the fire's out.

The publications mentioned in this essay are: *The Sugar Mile* (Picador, 2005); *Plays One: The Lifeblood, Wolfpit, The Only Girl in the World* (Oberon, 2005); *Plays Two: Broken Journey, Best Man Speech, The Last Valentine* (Oberon, 2006).

ℬ

Musarum Sacerdos:
An Interview With Michael Longley

Michael Longley's *Collected Poems* appeared this autumn. To mark the publication of this gravely beautiful book – the record of four decades of a practice which has helped keep lyric poetry in English both necessary and alive – *Poetry Review* asked the poet to put it in context.

The sheer substantiality of this Collected Poems, *set alongside the characteristic lucidity and concentration of your poems, seems almost paradoxical. So, despite the rehearsal of 1998's* Selected Poems, *it's all too easy to believe that the act of collection must have altered your relationship to individual poems. Is this, in fact, the case?*

I trust that in their new format the poems are more lucid and more concentrated. As I put the collection together I became aware of each poem as it related to others, and tried to treat the book as one long poem. I wanted an arrangement that felt organic. But that kind of editorial self-awareness could wreck future poems, and is now fading away. For me, orderliness and creativity don't go together. My *Collected Poems* is hardly massive (about the size of a novel), and that's a relief. I find doorstop collections disheartening.

What was *the editorial process?*

I photocopied all the poems and then did a scissors-and-paste job, keeping more or less to the order of each volume, and compromising between the beauty of a poem per page and the ugly practicality of running on. I tried to save space and create it. Ideally every poem should have its own page. (The test of a two-line poem is whether or not it fills the page.) In the new arrangement I wanted to give all the poems, especially the short ones, breathing space. I then photocopied the resulting sticky pages, and commissioned Gerry Hellawell of the Seamus Heaney Centre for Poetry to word-process the whole lot according to my page design. With me at her elbow we further explored patterns and adjusted the arrangement. Finally, *Collected Poems* was beamed through the ether as camera-ready copy.

Do you have strong views in general about the after-life of poems?

In my preliminary note I say that "by and large I prefer not to tinker with past efforts: this resembles denting cold metal that was red-hot in another life." I have cut out nine poems, excised stanzas from four, and altered a very few titles. I can think of hardly any poets whose revisions are improvements. The Muse is offended by face-lifts.

At a recent reading, it was pointed out to you that many of your audience were in tears. The Welsh call a particular kind of longing, perhaps for an archaic sense of home, hiraeth. *To what extent are you aware of – or intending to elicit – this kind of desire for an authentic return: in your readers or yourself? Is poetry, in other words, at all liturgical?*

The main problem is how to be private in public. I try to lose myself by giving voice to the poems as straightforwardly as possible. (My favourite poet-reader is Wallace Stevens.) Self-awareness or, worse, self-importance would be fatal for any reading and for my long-term artistic health. Tears and laughter are natural responses to art. So I was pleased to learn that my listeners had been moved. I must forget about that possibility before my next performance, and let the poems speak for themselves. Yes, the poet is *musarum sacerdos*, priest of the muses, or he is nothing. With its deepest roots in ceremony, poetry is sacerdotal: it commemorates and celebrates.

Is your relationship to landscape changing, as a collective consciousness of climate change takes root? Does the countryside seem, for example, more fragile; is it increasingly important to memorialise it?

Even my earliest landscape poems sound anxious. Now my so-called nature poems are prompted by despair as much as by delight. We are making such a mess of everything. In Ireland we are methodically turning beauty spots into eyesores. I memorialise lovely places as they disappear. Poetry gives things a second chance, perhaps now their only second chance. John Clare says, "Poets love nature and themselves are love."

Though you're famously a poet of Carrigskeewaun, the townland in the West of Ireland which has been your second home for several decades, you're also a poet of many other places: of Belfast, or of the death camps, for example. In Bartok's Mikrokosmos, *the miniatures encompass the composer's musical world but are also progressively more difficult to play. Do you have any analogous sense of lyric concentration as a training, a discipline?*

I have been going with my wife and children (and now grandchildren) to Carrigskeewaun for more than thirty years. It opens my eyes and keeps me alert, I hope, to the nuances of locality. I view all other places through the Mayo lens. I couldn't have written about Tuscany without years of trying to read the landscape around Carrigskeewaun. In one of my Mayo poems I say: "Home is a hollow between the waves, / A clump of nettles, feathery winds […]". The Famine-haunted fields remind me how provisional habitation is. And they help me to respond sensitively, I hope, to the desolation and abandonment of Terezin and Buchenwald.

One could imagine that "my Jewish granny" represents the sense of a joined-up world. Indeed, your Carrigskeewaun poems are frequently written to or from there (one thinks of the 'Letters' of An Exploded View; *the distance from and closeness to the late poet's New York in your elegy for Kenneth Koch). Visitors and family come and go – in two beautiful new poems which end the* Collected *it's your grandsons who visit – as if meaning-making, even in lyric verse, were collective.*

The central experiences in my life have been marriage and fatherhood and a few lasting friendships: naturally, these help to shape the plot of *Collected Poems*. But distant heroes and "everyday folk" also preoccupy me.

It pleases me that people come and go in my work. Poetry is communal as well as individual. Christopher Caudwell put it most profoundly when he wrote that "the instinctive ego of art is the common man into which we retire to establish contact with our fellows." And I love Donald Hall's definition of poetic tradition as "conversations with the dead great ones and with the living young." Poetry, even the most intensely lyrical, is unlikely to be a solo flight.

There's a particular sense that children make you vulnerable to the world in both the poems clustered round Gorse Fires's *'Ghetto' and – in another guise – in the earlier, almost-death-wishing and certainly Mahlerian, 'Kindertotenlieder'.*

I worried about everything much more as each of our three children was born. Surely everyone's the same? And now that we have four grandsons, well… I have written a poem for each of them – prayer, spell, lullaby, modes evolved by our ancestors.

Strikingly, given the orthodoxies which currently surround writing from material place, you also situate poems within the Classical tradition. From the 'Altera Cithera' of An Exploded View *to 'The Group', one of your latest poems, you signpost not so much classical myth as Greek and Roman writers* themselves. *Has writing 'after' such a tradition anything to do with diction, metre, prosody? Could you tell us a little about your relationship to a tradition (and wit – as in 'Damiana' –) which so unusually informs your lyric?*

When it comes to time, we are so parochial. Under the gaze of eternity Homer flourished only a blink ago. Ovid and Catullus are our near neighbours. Our civilisation is 70% Graeco-Roman (or more?). As an undergraduate I was obsessed with trying to write poetry and neglected my classical studies. In middle age I rediscovered Homer and, a little later, Ovid. Passages in the *Odyssey* enabled me to write belated lamentations for my parents and to broach nightmarish aspects of the Troubles. *The Iliad* is the greatest poem about war and death. Deep emotion and intellectual excitement draw me to certain passages which I feel compelled to respond to in an English version that "feels" like Homer (or Ovid). Diction, metre and prosody are far from being my main concerns. It is all much more uncertain and improvisatory and risky than those terms suggest. If this all sounds a bit long-faced, let me point out that 'The Group', for instance, and some of my other versions, are meant to be funny.

Could you say something about your musical influences, too?

I listen to music every day. It is central to my life. I have adored Sibelius since I was sixteen. But once I am concentrating, I have to turn such elemental surges down or off. The same applies to Mahler, Janacek, Berlioz, Ives and other favourites. Symphonic music burns up the oxygen in a small room. Sometimes I work with quieter sounds in the background - Angela Hewitt playing Couperin, Glenn Gould playing Bach's *The Well-Tempered Clavier*. The ghost of a third melody between left hand and right in Chopin and Schubert – I would love my lines to reverberate like that. Jazz (mostly from the twenties and thirties) can get me going – Bessie Smith's majesty, Fats Waller's combination of sunniness and subversion. I have wanted for years to write a poem about the white clarinetist Pee Wee Russell, but he keeps giving me the slip. I venerate the way he just about gets there after teetering on the edge of disaster. He makes me think again about what we mean by technique. Pee Wee lurks behind my line (from 'Praxilla'): "I subsist on fragments and improvisations." Although I know nothing about it technically, music means nearly as much to me as poetry. Listening to music and writing poetry connect for me at a deep level.

❧

Down To The Letter

ALEC PEEVER

Over the last fifteen years, the stone-carver Alec Peever has collaborated with contemporary poets, including Paul Muldoon, Mahmoud Darwish, Andrew Motion, Eilean ni Chuilleanain, Philip Gross, Yang Lian, at sites across the UK. Public Art has brought poetry to collective spaces – parks, city centres, shopping malls, cycle paths – where it might before have seemed counter-intuitive. More importantly, Peever practices an art of spatial, rather than simply contextual, translation. His work pays attention to the poems he works with; it traces their forms with a kind of creative fidelity (albeit across genres) which literary translators, editors – indeed all close readers – can recognise. More of his work can be seen on subsequent pages and at www.alecpeever.com

Yang Lian, *from* 'The Journey'

Introductions to Back In Print

The authors' Introductions to the first six volumes in the PBS *Back in Print* series give us a rare insight into what these poets – or in Geoffrey Hill's case his expert exegete, Jeffrey Wainwright – think now about key texts from among their earlier work. These insights are surprisingly intimate: they show us the books in the context of a writing life, as it has been lived both 'then' and 'now'. In the four we publish here, both Peter Porter and Penelope Shuttle revisit their poems in relation to the loss of a partner; Jeffrey Wainwright sees Geoffrey Hill's *The Triumph of Love* as a portrait of the artist as a young man; and Ruth Fainlight gives a vivid insight into artistic collaboration and the processes of revision which a new edition can entail.

℘

Sibyls And Others
Ruth Fainlight

It must have been some time in the 1970s when, knowing that I was interested in such matters, the American artist Leonard Baskin suggested we work together on a book of poems and drawings based on the subject of Sibyls, those prophetic women of the ancient world. I did not realise that my acceptance would mark a decisive change in how I worked and what I wrote about. It was the first time I would research a subject specifically for a sequence of poems, and my first experience of an artistic collaboration. Since then, I have worked with several other artists, as well as composers and a film-maker, but this book was my introduction to the inspirations and constraints of that situation. In fact, the proposed book never appeared. The pen and ink and wash drawings were exhibited, sold, dispersed. Unfortunately, I had kept no photographic record of them. But I could not regret my involvement. It had been a thrilling experience, and produced the twenty-seven poems which are the first part of this book. (Years later, Leonard approached me again for Sibyl poems. He had returned to the subject and made a dozen powerful woodcuts. This time, he promised, a book would result. I was reluctant at first, then had to respond to such strong images – and the twelve poems I wrote became the text for a splendid folio of prints and poems, published in a limited edition in the early 1990s.)

Reading this collection again has been an interesting experience. I could also characterise it as daunting, disconcerting and occasionally gratifying. Daunting: did I really write so many poems during those few years – poems I thought good enough to include in a collection (where many others were either discarded or never completed)? Disconcerting: is that what I really thought and felt then? Gratifying: but how long might I continue to feel that they expressed my thoughts and emotions and had some value? The last time I read the book attentively was when preparing my second *Selected Poems*, which appeared in 1995 and draws on work from eight collections published between 1966 and 1990. *Sibyls and Others*, 1980, is number five in the sequence. I chose few poems from the first collections – four from the first, eight from the second, the number increasing only slowly with each. But after the fourth book, a higher proportion of the contents passed the test of acceptability. There was no doubt that the complete Sibyl sequence must be used, and from the rest of the contents of that volume – the *Others* – I chose about one in three. Now, after more than a quarter of a century, the entire collection is being brought back to life.

One of the most interesting aspects of the re-reading was to discover how many of the poems were altered for the *Selected* – something I had entirely forgotten. Most changes were to lineation and punctuation: there were lines which seemed to end in the wrong place and words pointlessly carried over; nor did I like, by the use of a semi-colon or a dash, to create a heavier pause or more definite break in or between lines than I now thought appropriate. ('Now' in this case meaning then, when I was preparing the 1995 volume, even though the changes might have been made a year or two earlier; I remember working on that *Selected* for a considerable time.) A few of the alterations were so major that about a dozen poems were more or less re-written rather than simply corrected. In 1995 I believed I was altogether more skilful than when I had written the originals. *Now* (which means the moment of writing this introduction in 2006), that conviction, and those alterations and choices, give me cause to ponder. How can I know whether my changes made the poems better or worse? Impossible to decide. And tempting though it is to put the entire collection through yet another revision, I shall resist. Apart from one or two minor changes to poems not included in the *Selected* and therefore unaltered since first publication in 1980, this book is as close to the original *Sibyls and Others* as I can allow.

The Cost of Seriousness
Peter Porter

*T*he Cost of Seriousness, which was published first in 1978, stands at the crux of my lifetime's work in poetry. Though not my personal favourite among my books (that would be *Preaching To The Converted* of 1972), it is certainly the most admired by readers, and marks a crisis in my writing life, and may be said to divide my early maturity from my more arcane consolidation of the last three decades.

The book's controlling theme is a lament for my first wife, Jannice, who died in unhappy circumstances at the end of 1974. This is developed in direct laments – 'An Exequy' and 'The Delegate' – and more glancingly in 'The Easiest Room in Hell', 'An Angel in Blythburgh Church' and 'Evensong'. Other poems group around these elegies and maintain a tone of sadness and regret, whether dealing with European Art and History or a sense of detritus recalled from early life in Australia.

In some ways this collection is a crossroads between a somewhat neurotic subjectivity and a recovered objectivity. It is technically less audacious than some of my other books perhaps, but more of a piece than most.

Alec Peever, Paul Muldoon, 'The Breather' for Salisbury Festival

Adventures With My Horse
Penelope Shuttle

So what sort of Adventures was I having, back in 1988, and with what Horse? The Adventures were the travels and questions of Imagination through the world, and the Horse was (and still is) Poetry, one of the Pegasus breed. My Horse permitted me to ride. He is a horse no-one can break in, but he will *allow* you to ride.

Our Adventures were manifold. We explored the electricity and energy-fields of sexual love; we trudged through the desolation world described in the poem 'Thief', where "...you go nakedly through the skyless moonless gardens and pagodas/of envy...". We were entertained, my Horse and I, by the lifestyles of other animals, pigs, snakes, cows, foxes, swans.

Thanks to my vantage on the back of my Horse, I was able to explore God, landscape and memory.

My Horse is also, in the title poem itself, a way of describing my unconceived son, a theme I've pursued in various poems. My unconceived son belongs, of course, in the category of "the road not taken". The child who is never conceived is a presence that haunts the poems of this time, when I was still of an age when I could indeed have had a second child. Here I am, thinking about him –

> If the boy is a horse, who rides him?
> He is a boy when he fears the night,
> He is a horse when morning comes [...]

Sometimes this boy plays at being a horse; sometimes he is seen by the mother in the poem like this:

> His rough-maned head glows in windswept sunlight [...]

The poem is a working-out of the relationship between mother and son; it acts as a mirror in which I can see a life-path I did not take. And the sadness, the loss involved, is mediated by language which is, as Robert Graves remarks, like the burnished shield Perseus holds up against the Gorgon, a protected way of seeing things that otherwise are destructive to the self.

The book concludes with my longest poem to date – 'Clayman, Leatherman, Glassman'. Looking back, this reads to me as words to an as-yet-uncomposed oratorio. It tells the story of three craftsmen who, at the prompting of three powerful female spirits or Eves, each make a woman –

out of clay, out of leather, and out of glass. But it is the female spirits who preside and direct the action.

This poem was influenced profoundly by living in Cornwall, a county with more visual artists resident within its borders than any other area in England, after London. Peter [Redgrove] and I often used to visit a craft centre over on The Lizard, where we watched the craftspeople at work, potters, leatherworkers, and glass-makers. We saw them at all stages of their work, and it was this experience that led me to write this creation story-poem.

However, there is one poem I find hard to read in this collection written by my younger self. This line from 'The Living', which had slipped from my mind for years, shocks me now –

>   she wakes to all the white news of grief –

 for that *white news* has occupied me greatly since I lost Peter in the summer of 2003.

But it is also important for me to set beside that static of grief the recollection of the happy productive years we shared. *Adventures With My Horse* is proof of those years.

Alec Peever, Andrew Motion, 'Flint' for Salisbury Festival

Geoffrey Hill's *The Triumph of Love*
Jeffrey Wainwright

The one hundred and fifty poem sequence of *The Triumph of Love* (1998) is neither narrative nor mindscape but nevertheless offers frequent glimpses of the narrator: "I speak / deliberately like an old man who last saw it - / Romsley – through a spinning bike-wheel" (LXXXII). Romsley, "spraddled ridge- / village", is the same home territory of *Mercian Hymns* (1971) and the boy who appears there is recognisable in these new details: listening to the wireless, reading *Radio Fun,* poring over his aircraft recognition cards, convincing himself of the respective capabilities of the Fairey Battle and Swordfish, seeing a warship in a water tower and the distant but awesome spectacle of the bombing of Coventry: "huge silent whumphs / of flame-shadow bronzing the nocturnal / cloud-base of her now legendary dust" (VII).

The sequence begins and ends in Romsley – "Guilts were incurred in that place" (II) - and everything between is seen as through the refracting whirr of that "spinning bike-wheel". The war and its aftermath and memory (Hill was born in 1932) is central. Homage is paid, horror and waste described, bitterness, restrained and unrestrained, poured forth. The speaker is also "an obstinate old man", "a rancorous old sod", and his tones are widely satirical and caustic, even recklessly unlovely. These moods of the poem are meant to discomfit the reader and they do whether through spleen, or the demands that have his imaginary sub gasping to explicate his uncompromising world of reference, or gloss his Latin: "["Strewth!!! "already present in time as in nature"? – ED]" (CXXV).

But, as here, there is self-mockery too, and a wonderful sense of comedy both in beautifully phrased appreciations of Laurel and Hardy "cutting, pacing, repacing, their / flawless shambles", and in his own wordplay. Within the cycle too is great reverence for heroes, and humility. And finally there is love, wrung against pain, as in one of the mercurial and beautiful hymns to his *Vergine bella*, the female figure of grace Hill derives from Petrarch's own *Trionfo d'Amore*: a prayer to her "commits and commends us to loving / desperately, yet not with despair, not / even in desperation."

☙

Company of Loners:
The *Workshop Gen* Poets

C. L. DALLAT

Michael Donaghy, after one of our regular workshops at either Robert Greacen's place in Notting Hill or Matthew Sweeney's Holborn environs, argued persuasively that poetry was the most immediate, most unmediated, most exposing of arts. Unlike the composer who can only fully communicate his ideas, his creativity, through one hundred and twenty seven orchestral musicians and a conductor – unlike the dramatist who requires producers, directors, angels, stage-hands, a ticket office and a cast of several, at least, to see his thoughts, narratives and observations conceived – the poet has merely, in his stereotypical garret, to put pencil to paper and art exists.

That 'unmediated artist' vision of the isolated, independent garret-genius practising a tool-less and subvention-free trade gives insufficient recognition, however, to the very fact that our post-workshop debates (on writing, reading, Rushdie, poll-tax, elitism, the meaning of life, the death of post-modernism...) owed their existence to our gathering for mutual improvement: in a communal exercise dignified by the '50s & '60s vogue for 'groups' (beat groups, group theatre, women's groups, group therapy) and the '70s substitution of 'workshop' as intrinsically more purposeful, more artisanal and less feeling-centred. Indeed the famous 'Group', under Philip Hobsbaum and, later, Edward Lucie-Smith, had become variously the 'Writers' Workshop' or the 'Poets' Workshop' – according to different accounts – by 1965. Interestingly the term before 'The Group' was 'The Movement', a term too redolent of pre-war mass movements (from scouting to Dagenham Girl Pipers to Hitler Youth) to have survived long in the liberal arts; but which nonetheless avoided the unseemly early prevalence of '-isms' where, post-Symbolism, Moscow's Futurists gathered at the Tower while the Acme-ists met at the Stray Dog, with an unbridgeable Prospekt between.

The fact that poets gather to share poems does not, of itself, prove that the verdict of one's peers is essential to the offspring of solitary genius. The observation that those who gathered in this workshop over a five or six year period (some throughout, some only briefly) – Matthew Sweeney, Lavinia Greenlaw, Maurice Riordan, Ruth Padel, Don Paterson, Vicki Feaver, Jo Shapcott, Katherine Gallagher, Charles Boyle, Sarah Maguire, Tim Dooley,

Eva Salzman and the late and much missed Michael Donaghy – went on to be some of the most significant and most influential poets of the past decade certainly could, however, be read as suggesting that sharing work, advice, criticism, theory and, occasionally, Fitou, had some impact on the world of contemporary poetry.

But if the group took on board poets as diverse as the roster above – Donaghy's metaphysics struggling with cosmopolite Bronx realities; Padel's classicism giving way to visceral, emotional free-wheeling; Maguire's botanical detachment overwhelmed by responses to Middle East politics, say – and produced poets whose work, directions, underlying principles even, are as different as they are today, what then is a workshop, a group, a school without an '-ism', for?

It may be easier to say what this workshop was against. It was, collectively, against adjectives; against unearned metaphor; against the limp, domestic cameo; against the working-up of an unusual historical fact of no intrinsic relevance, considered post-Muldoon a circus trick; against translating history/scripture/myth into the contemporary if the poet or reader didn't consequently engage with the narrative; against trendiness. And if quoting Yeats, paraphrasing Heaney, punning on Eliot, weren't exactly frowned upon, they were never thought adequate.

No rules; but one consensus was that nothing was beneath poetry. Sweeney, in an interview I wrote up for *Verse* in 1992, excoriated a negative review which chided him for merely mentioning subjects as 'unpoetic' as hitch-hiking and takeaways. And there was a sense that poetry shouldn't merely address an audience who shared core cultural values. Thus the *roman* that relied on the *clef* was little liked: the fact that by the end no-one had realised the poem was actually about Dante's Beatrice, Van Gogh's Dr. Gachet, Sarah Kane's *Blasted* or Ferdinand de Lesseps and the Suez Canal was guaranteed not to impress even when the explanation came.

And the jury remained hung on whether that openness to contemporary matter took one down the road of demotic speech and free verse or 'back' to traditional form.

If there was a purpose to these sundry prohibitions and forswearings it was an underlying conviction that poetry must be, or must remain, widely accessible, without becoming easy or lazy or predictable: and that the glaring gap between the most popular and the most stringent would not be resolved by taking one side or another.

There were, inevitably, overlapping themes. Thatcherism, for one. Greacen, born before Ireland was divided, and a pre-war member of the Peace Pledge Union (along with Glens of Antrim poet-and-socialist, John Hewitt), remained an avowedly political poet, and the only writer from a

North of Ireland background who has probed, in 'A Garland for Captain Fox', the deep-seated empathy between the Intelligence community, financial elites and publicly-unpopular Unionism: Sweeney's 'No Answer' satirises the Iron Lady's relationship with Reagan but 'To the Building Trade' has an altogether more ground-level take on the monetarist era's excesses. Varieties of twentieth century popular music inevitably recurred, too. And there was an obsession with food: Sweeney is a superb cook and a gastronome, yet it is Riordan's 'Fish' that remains the perfect essay on metaphor. Padel had 'Summer Snow' and Boyle, 'Snow in September'; Boyle's de Chirico surrealism in 'The Chess Player' found an echo in/of Riordan's deserted Mahonesque cities; Riordan and Sweeney both noticed cacti; Donaghy's musical and intellectual precision resonates with Greenlaw's and Riordan's 'scientific' explorations while his musical eclecticism – Purcell, Mozart, legendary accordionists in Jimmy-the-Priest's, Nafthule Bradndwein's Klezmer Orchestra, Bechet's 'enormous yes' – paralleled some of my own poetic and musical obsessions.

There were subtle cross-fertilisations too: did Greenlaw's 'The Man Whose Smile Made Medical History' and Shapcott's 'Electroplating the Baby' provide the impetus for Sweeney's 'Artificial Blood', or was it the other way round? Certainly a growing interest in things askew and bizarre led to *Emergency Kit: Poems for Strange Times*, Sweeney and Shapcott's take on a world of just-controlled weirdness. And Padel's early workshop subject, 'On the Venom Farm', can be seen as prefiguring her interest in metaphorical, literal and potentially fatal forms of wildlife.

Then there were the parallel lives. Donaghy's imagined brother; Boyle's character who would have lived in Crawley; Riordan's 'realtor Charlie Flitcraft' who walked off, like Muldoon's Brownlee or a character in some '40s movie; and Sweeney's travelling husband who spends half the week in his 'shadow home'. (Is disappearing, being someone else, a male obsession, perhaps?) Riordan even noted, at a recent Coffee-House Poetry reading at the Troubadour (the venue where, along with Bernard Stone's Holborn bookshop, workshop members were most likely to have London launches) that his 'A Word from the Loki' and Donaghy's 'Shooting The Crane People' shared the same anthropologically distancing tone without either poet's having read the other work. That evening's reminiscing was noteworthy, too, for the fact that none of the readers expressed diffidence about being identified with the workshop, a disavowal familiar from attempts to define Hobsbaum's famous 'Belfast Group', where some poets are keen to point out that they only went along 'once or twice'.

Danger was a theme which also cropped up regularly in the workshop's poems: from Vicki Feaver's 'The Handless Maiden' and 'Wood Pigeon' to sundry knives and guns in Sweeney's magical-surrealism narratives to Boyle's *noir*-ish 'I Didn't Mean to Kill My Husband'. Knives were, in fact, hard to avoid: as the workshop's method of selecting which anonymous stack of a dozen copies would be workshopped next was a kitchen knife, spun roulette style and coming to rest on the next lucky supplicant. And in that simple ritual lay, arguably, the workshop's strength and its weakness.

My other group, The Poetry Workshop, (joined in the year before I met Matthew Sweeney and Robert Greacen at a Kavanagh twentieth-anniversary celebration at the Almeida), was a distant relation, several times removed, of the Hobsbaum 'Group'; and followed (I was told) the Group's *modus* of focusing on one writer's work each month, requiring commitment for the eight out of every nine months in which you didn't get to bring any of your own work, and dispensing with anonymity as a body of material was circulated in advance. That led to criticism contextualised against what had been brought before, one's known voice, one's progress in various directions... The anonymous reading of ten to twelve sets of poems under the Greacen/Sweeney rules, the referee allowing just fifteen minutes for each poem, militated against long work, against work seen in the context of the writer's development, against self-referentiality, against the sort of prior knowledge of a writer that the general reader acquires having bought a poetry book and read the biographical details, or having encountered a name more than once in small magazines.

The workshop's high time coincided with the birth of the *Independent* and its daily poems which, like recordings geared for sales (and therefore expecting promotion in a popular medium), were usually moderately accessible and invariably of standardised length. The '80s were as much the era of the under-30-line poem as the '60s were for the three-minute single. The incidence of long poems in workshop members' subsequent collections actually probably tends towards a notional national average: the number of long poems brought to the workshop, however, (one striking exception being Don Paterson's 'The Alexandrian Library'), was comparable to the number of over-ten-minute singles on Capital Gold. And a two-liner, however terse, was as unlikely to sustain a quarter-hour's exegesis as it was to win an Arvon or National Prize. Thus the workshop can, *inter alia*, be credited, or blamed, for promoting work that was not only accessible but manageable, containable, and capable of appearing in a national newspaper, in the midst of a *New Yorker* article, or in a literary journal without taking up half the magazine.

Somewhere around 1992, however – with increasing recognition for most of its poets, with the inevitable stresses and strains between conflicting theories on how to renew popular poetry without easy populism, and with the sweeping up of some of its number into that other, albeit artificial, team, *New Gen* (and, much later, *Next Gen*) – the enterprise folded quietly: no scroll, no year-book, no 'Girl Most Likely To Succeed', no strawberries. But the fruits of perhaps six or seven years of endeavour arising from an alliance between two Irish literary exiles – one who was post-Tom-Waits, one who knew Noël Coward – are very much present in the poetry written and read today; and in the work of an upcoming generation who are no doubt even now inviting each new and startling poetic acquaintance to gather somewhere and have their poems workshopped, literally at knife-point.

Alec Peever, *from* 'Wye', Riverside Park, High Wycombe

REVIEWS

Death is the most ruthless of all editors.
—Patrick Crotty

The Pastoral Is Political

ADAM THORPE

Michael Longley, *Collected Poems*, Cape, hb. £25, ISBN 9780224079273

Michael Longley is a nature poet in the tradition of John Clare and Edward Thomas, a debt he openly repays in his verse: in the recent 'Edward Thomas's Poem', the Belfast poet fails to "make out the miniscule handwriting" in the war notebook, but imagines Thomas in the trenches hearing "the skylark's / Skyward exultation". Clare appears in Longley's first collection, *No Continuing City* (1969), as a ditch-dwelling escapee from the asylum, "my head low as / a lark's nest", intent on a project of ecological recuperation.

In another earlyish poem, the witty 'Options', Longley explicitly identifies himself alongside the mad Clare, "Siphoning through the ears / Letters of the alphabet / And, with the vowels and consonants, / My life of make-believe". Both Clare and Thomas hallowed the "miniscule", the observed detail; exultation had to be earned through the particular, not the romantic generalities of a Schiller. Exultation is wordless but can be embodied, usually after much effort, in the lyric line, in the siphoning and sieving of syllables. This has always been Longley's meticulous project; and here are four decades' worth of poems to prove it, running from his early formalism to the spare eloquence of *Snow Water* (2004).

For much of that forty-year period, the context has been darkened by the Northern Irish conflict: war (as one side termed it) of a peculiarly domestic but typically gruesome kind. One of the under-sung triumphs of contemporary poetry has been its ability to respond to that conflict in all its complexity and contradiction and ugliness, and Longley has consistently proved himself one of its finest elegists. Lament is the keynote, grounded in identifiable victims: a bus-conductor shot in his carpet-slippers in front of the television; three off-duty policemen out fishing; the ice-cream man, with his flavours which Longley memorably sets beside the names of flowers, as if some natural law has been broken. He has the even-handedness of someone who abhors violence and sectarianism: in the celebrated 'Wounds', it is three teenage British soldiers with "bellies full of / Bullets and Irish beer" who are buried in his imagination alongside his father, a veteran of the trenches who appears again and again as a fleshly revenant alongside the murdered with their "spectacles, wallets, small change[…]".

Longley was trained as a classicist, and his response to the Ceasefire was a retake on the *Iliad*, where Achilles and Priam are impossibly reconciled after the death of Hector:

> I get down on my knees and do what must be done
> And kiss Achilles' hand, the killer of my son.

'Ceasefire', published in the *Irish Times*, was a somewhat public poem, which perhaps explains the uncharacteristic rhythm of that last couplet. Longley is generally understated and subtle in the movement of his verse; to the point where some of his short poems can seem to melt away at the edges, snow sculptures to which we've come just too late in the thaw. This is the Japanese and Chinese influence, perhaps, most provokingly evident in the title poem of *The Weather in Japan* (2000), a brief couplet reminiscent of Pound's imagism:

> *The Weather In Japan*
>
> Makes bead curtains of the rain,
> Of the mist a paper screen.

Elsewhere, this kind of risky evanescence is offset by startlingly evocative images – the frozen waterfall "a chandelier"; a herd's hoof-prints "watermarks under all that we say"; ice preventing a robin "ripening on its branch". He is also, it must be said, a witty poet, with a line in self-effacing put-downs born perhaps from his years as an Arts Council Director.

The *Odyssey* is a repeated literary refuge, and Longley is always coming home – to Carrigskeewaun. This village and its "commonage" on the coast of County Mayo harbour all the mysteries Longley needs: the flowers, the animals, the sea. He has provocatively called his nature poems his "most political": and not just because "I want the light from Carrigskeewaun to irradiate the northern darkness". The world's troubles go beyond war to the existential question of how to live "with the plants and the other animals". War is an evasion of this central question, as are pseudo-ecological schemes to relieve us of responsibility rather than catastrophe. Longley's poems return us to the natural matter of otters, sanderlings, seals. Increasingly, it seems enough just to watch, to observe, to take in: "I should have spent my life / Listening to the waves," he remarks, in typically rueful mood. Longley is fascinated by the relationship between the name and the named, and has a medieval's fondness for lists. In his softly-spoken readings, names of flowers become reverential talismans.

The sanderling, or sand piper, breeds on the northern tundra, and

Longley is haunted by this icy hint of elsewhere, as he is haunted by death (including the industrialised version, the "tangled pile", of the camps). Death, however, is allayed by conjuring it in effigy: from 'Three Posthumous Pieces' to the well-known 'Detour' – in which he brilliantly imagines his own funeral passing "Down the single street of a small market town" and bringing him face to face with "grubby parsnips" and "gas cylinders" – he blurs the distinctions between being and not-being, as he does when he imagines himself absent from his parents' early lives. Memories and ghosts are of the same stuff, death "no more than / An exhalation".

At a more physical level, he seems to be saying, an individual's earthly span melds into the natural cycle of migratory and weather patterns; an otter glimpsed in the sea; "a haze of hawkbit"; or the ancient burial mound that appears again and again as a kind of nodal reference point (he himself wishes to be buried where the mountain hare licks "snow stains from her underside"). Similarly, the body itself becomes indistinguishable from water in the many poems that feature skinny-dipping: one of the earliest poems, 'Nausicaa' ("The ocean gathers where your shoulder turns") is echoed some thirty years later in 'Sandpiper', in which a pool shared with the animals and insects was where "we made out of shoulders and shins our cataract".

Ultimately, the lyric impulse is to match both what we witness, as well as what we feel, with an intense moment (or permanent artefact) of language, a kind of spell or evocation in which onomatopoeia plays an underrated (because so-called primitive) part – from the "galvanised aeolian gate" to "the duach's sheepbitten edge". At times, Longley's lines melt into their own dogged music, so that they become sound-objects, as collectible as pebbles – achieving a pebble's essential meaninglessness not through Swinburnian vapidness but by being nothing more than a film or 'meniscus' over their natural subject. This is probably the ultimate achievement for a lyric poet of Longley's intensity: that a line needs no justification other than itself – a reprise of the ultimate meaning of the natural world.

Adam Thorpe's next collection is *Birds With A Broken Wing* (Cape, 2007).

Hard, Beautiful Truths

JAY PARINI

Tomas Tranströmer, versions by Robin Robertson, *The Deleted World*,
Enitharmon, £8.95, ISBN 1904634486;
Don Paterson, *Orpheus: A Version of Rilke's Die Sonette an Orpheus*,
Faber, hb. £12.99, ISBN 0571222684

Poetry is what is found in translation. That is, poets translate from silence itself, finding a language adequate to their experience, moving yet another fragment of the unsaid into "said" territory. Translations from other languages, whether (as in this case) Swedish or German, merely extend the range of these discoveries, at least in the best examples. These two volumes of translations, modestly called "versions" by their authors, represent the activity well, as both are by poets who understand that the first duty of the translator is to create a "version" that stands on its own as a poem in English.

Tomas Tranströmer is one of the finest poets in Sweden. For half a century, he has been publishing enigmatic, evocative poems that underline an almost occult sense of the relationship between words and things. He is a quiet poet, attuned to the slight shifts of weather and geography that, as metaphors, represent minute adjustments of mood and, in a larger sense, spirit.

What I love about Tranströmer is the way he explores language itself as a metaphor, as in 'From March 1979', taken from this new volume:

> Sick of those who come with words, words but no language,
> I make my way to the snow-covered island.
>
> Wilderness has no words. The unwritten pages
> stretch out in all directions.
>
> I come across this line of deer-slots in the snow: a language,
> language without words.

This archetypal poem forms a tiny myth, describing a literal journey with symbolic dimensions, thus extending the metaphor in various directions. Most of us who read a good deal are sick of those "who come with words, words but no language." This revulsion often propels a poem into being, as in Yeats's "I will arise and go now, and go to Innisfree." One arrives in the land of silence: "Wilderness has no words." The metaphor rapidly becomes a conceit, as the unprinted fields of snow become "unprinted pages." The sleight of mind in the last stanza is, again, typical: Tranströmer deepens the image unexpectedly, giving a literal level – the deer's footprints in the snow – and a range of associations, as we are left contemplating this "language without words" – which (in my own association) is akin to Chomsky's Universal Grammar – which underlies speech, underwrites silence itself.

A sensuous and concrete poet himself, Robin Roberston does a fine job of creating versions of Tranströmer that stand on their own as poems in English. They are deftly musical, with phrases ringing in the ear after the page is turned, as in the last stanza of 'A Winter Night':

> A darker storm stands over the world.
> It puts its mouth to our soul
> and blows to get a tone. We are afraid
> the storm will blow us empty.

Even with the Swedish version staring at me across the page, I cannot judge how well Robertson has translated the original; but I know he has given us a gift in English, and one for which I, for one, will remain grateful. This strikes me as one of Tranströmer's strongest collections, and we're lucky that Roberston has taken to it so keenly, adjusting his own ear to the ear of the target poems, taking deep soundings in their chilly depths.

Don Paterson, another gifted poet, has turned to one of the most translated sequences of our time, the *Sonnets to Orpheus* of Rilke. This was a bold move, as Rilke is notoriously impossible to translate. Robert Lowell, who wrestled himself with Rilke, once said that it was almost impossible to imagine him in English, as his poems were sealed in German. Unsealing Rilke has become a minor industry over the decades since the *Sonnets to Orpheus* first appeared in 1922.

I have long admired the much-abused early translation of the sonnets by J.B. Leishman (1936), which Stepher Spender later reworked with varying degrees of success. In the forties, C.F. Macintyre offered a sturdy alternative to Leishman. Among many translators, Stephen Mitchell (1985) – well-known for his version of the *Tao Te Ching* – has done a splendid version of the sonnets, although everything Mitchell does sounds vaguely like Pablo Neruda in California. There was a marvellous version of the sequence by David Young, himself a good poet, in the late eighties. Only a couple of years ago, Edward Snow – a professor in Texas – published a vigorous, quite literal, translation.

But Paterson's Rilke is, for me, the best version to appear thus far, giving a concreteness to the poems that most earlier translations lack. It's easy to get lost in the huge mist of language sprayed by Rilke, with those oratorical flourishes that just don't work in English, as in the famous opening lines of the first sonnet: "*Da stieg ein Baum. O reine Übersteigung! / O Orpheus singt! O hoher Baum im Ohr!*" Paterson translates as follows: "A tree rose from the earth. O pure transcendence – / Orpheus sings: O tall oak in the ear!" The English-tuned ear cringes slightly, as it must, at such a line as "O pure transcendence." *Übersteigung* contains within it both "transcendence" and "ascendance" in German (the word derives from *steigen*, "to climb"), hence it exudes a double valence that cannot easily be accommodated in English. But the Paterson version works well, as in the second line the addition of "earth" (not in Rilke) lends a spatial sense to the image that quietly underscores "transcendence," making it more visual, if not quite literal.

Throughout these sonnets, Paterson consistently adds a concrete element to the language, admitting an earthiness that the German lacks. One further example will illustrate this. In the late poem in the sequence that begins "*Zwischen den Steren, wie weit...*", the poet contemplates the distances between stars and the vaster distances that occur between people, as between one child and another: "O how ineffably far." This later version is a more literal version, as translated by Edward Snow. Paterson does this with the stanza:

> From star to star – such distances: and yet
> those encountered here are harder reckoned.
> Someone – a child, say, and then a second...
> What dark matter holds them separate?

There is no "dark matter" in Rilke. But Paterson's addition gives the line a freshness and contemporaenity that it lacks in the more literal version. It is also intriguing: the vast distance between two human beings characterized as a kind of negative space. The poem unspools to the end in a fresh, concrete way by adding elements not found in the German text, as when Rilke writes about the strangeness of a table laid with a plate of fish. Paterson writes: "How strange the eyes and dead mouths of the fish." Those eyes and mouths are Paterson's alone.

Rilke wrote the *Sonnets to Orpheus* only four years before his death. It was composed as an elegy of sorts for a teenager of his acquaintance, Vera Knoop, whose mother was an old friend. He had recently been sent a package by Vera's mother that contained a sixteen-page chronicle of her daughter's death by leukemia, and this prompted the sonnets, which were written in a blaze of thirteen days. As a whole, the sequence praises and rues the endless flux of the universe, its transformations (death being only one stage in a cycle that inevitably points to rebirth). Orpheus, as the prototype of the poet, visited the realm of death, and miraculously returned to tell the tale; by implication, poets do likewise. In their brightest moments, Rilke's sonnets celebrate the hard, beautiful truths pried loose as from silence itself, in the tenth sonnet:

> I praise all things wrested from doubt,
> Those mouths alive with their new voice
> having learnt the truth of silence.

Jay Parini, a poet and novelist, most recently published *The Art Of Subtraction: New And Selected Poems* (Braziller, 2005).

Watch out for...

the announcement of the 2006
Geoffrey Dearmer Prize winner in the next issue of
Poetry Review, 97:1, Spring 2007

Rabbits And Bastards

DAVID MORLEY

Alan Brownjohn, *Collected Poems*, Enitharmon, hb. £25.00,
ISBN 9781904634218

Poets rarely visited Blackpool when I was growing up there and, if they chanced to, they did not give readings: for if poetry is the opposite of money, Blackpool was the opposite of poetry venue. So when Alan Brownjohn showed up to read at the Central Library in the early 1980s we all gawped as if he'd escaped from the zoo or stepped from one of the glowing star-ships that adorned The Illuminations. It was like the scene in his poem 'We are going to see the rabbit...':

> Which rabbit?
> The only rabbit,
> The only rabbit in England
> Sitting behind a barbed-wire fence
> Under the floodlights, neon lights...
> On the only patch of grass
> In England...

Or so it seemed to us in the poet-free zone called Blackpool where the coin arcade was our teenage culture choice. I admit we were not at his reading "in thousands" but we hoped for illumination and Brownjohn lent it and left something behind in several of us (for there were a few of us starting out as young writers). What he lent was the idea that there were patches of grass in our culture; places and stays where poetry could exist, despite the neon-lit social pressure to chase cash and cut a living. I gave up my part-time job as a bingo-caller, and started writing instead.

The poets who influence us are like heroic teachers. Their influence takes the form of a series of one-sided marriages, but one where the new writer keeps the house as it were. I learnt that imitating a poet with a dense or highly distinct voice (say Hughes, Plath, Dylan Thomas) closes down your own possibilities if you do not possess the articulate cunning to escape their stylistic force-field. There's nothing wrong in sounding roughly the same as the poets you admire (your critics will smile at the head-start this gives them), but imitation can be nine-tenths limitation. However, Brownjohn's visit seeded an idea that if you are starting out (as many readers of poetry and poetry magazines are), it seems a good idea to sample styles of writing that are plain, clear, or which simply do not possess linguistically nervous tics. Alan Brownjohn's *Collected Poems*, beautifully produced by Enitharmon, is worth your time for many reasons; not least what it can teach. Its clear, precise suite of styles, especially across the length of the sequences; his fascinating use of fiction in poems; and what Sean O'Brien calls his "mesmeric, meditative pace, and a consistently dramatic mode, surely related to the strategies of the classroom" (Brownjohn was a teacher) create open spaces for readerly and writerly engagement.

Like O'Brien (who I suspect is influenced by him) Brownjohn is a careful and secular moralist in his verse; and, like O'Brien, his stanzas never become little nanny-states with palpable designs on the reader (although that risk is always there in both poets). The care is in the observed detail, which is often minute in its attention. We squirm with the bandmaster among the officers, our "eyes always going to the face speaking next" in the much-anthologised 'Class Incident from Graves', while,

> The band put away their instruments out at the back, having
> Drunk their beers, standing.

How much observed and obsessive social tension is there in that single word *standing*. You could build a revolution on it, but we don't do those in Britain.

To return to the Blackpool where business was a kind of necessary art form (as the poet Richard Hugo once said of his own experience in post-war America): Alan Brownjohn is merciless about such matters, and the fierce natural selection of money-making processes. His poem against business mentality is tenderly titled 'Bastard', and should be compulsory reading for all of us who imagine we are not. For Brownjohn, "The Bastard is full of fear and fantasy, / And the fantasy that made his world for him / Becomes a fantastic fear of losing it [...]". But our smiling friend does lose it, in both senses, and loses his world in a speech against the shareholders:

> 'I've sussed it out – you're just a lot of *bastards,*
> A lot of dirty, crooked, scheming *bastards!*'

> When the door slams hard behind him, they look at each other
> And shake their heads with humane and pitying smiles.
> 'Poor bastard', one compassionately murmurs.

Humane and pitying smiles. A fantastic fear of losing it. How devastatingly accurate in all its plain, clear, open language. Alan Brownjohn is far fiercer than his care and attention make him out to be, and a wonderful poet whose lifetime attention to verse is celebrated by this very solid *Collected*. What a pity, in some ways, he was never part of a real government as well as a government of the tongue (he was once a labour councillor and a parliamentary candidate). What would the acknowledged legislations of such a poet look like?

David Morley's 'The Charges On Midsummer Night For The Coventry Mysteries' appears on p. 32.

❧

Thinking Back

STEVEN MATTHEWS

Ed. Douglas Dunn, *Twentieth Century Scottish Poetry*, Faber, £12.99
ISBN 9780571228386;
Ed. Paul Muldoon, *Contemporary Irish Poetry*, Faber, £12.99
ISBN 9780571228379

What is going on at Faber Poetry? After a decade and more in which the imprint has noticeably failed to foster new talent (although one in which it has been noticeably canny in acquiring talent fostered elsewhere, as in the aftermath of the collective moment of madness by the Oxford University Press delegates), there come these reprinted anthologies. The editorial decision behind their re-appearance is truly strange. Both volumes are unedited republications of books that appeared originally in 1986, in the case of the Muldoon, 1992/3 of the Dunn. Nothing, so far as I can see, has been altered in either case. There seems to have been no request to Muldoon or Dunn to update their selections, or to consider adding new names to the lists of the anthologised, or perhaps to remove others. What we have in each book, then, are curiously time-locked productions which now seem remote from current debates around what used to be called regionalism and the centre, margins and mainstream, modernism and modernity, in poetry.

Think back, if you can, to a time before the Anglo-Irish Agreement, let alone before the cessation of violence and a degree of all-Ireland government in the north of Ireland; think back to a time before the limited devolution for Scotland created by the Blair government. Think back to a time when Seamus Heaney had not long published *Station Island*; a time before Derek Mahon had produced his verse letters in couplets, before Michael Longley had produced his versions from Homer, or Medbh McGuckian *On Ballycastle Beach* (let alone her masterwork *Shelmalier*). To a time when young Don Paterson had only published *Nil Nil*, Carol Ann Duffy had only got as far as *Another Country,* John Burnside as *The Hoop*, Robert Crawford to *A Scottish Assembly* and *Sharawaggi.* And there you are in the time-world of these unevolved anthologies.

A curious decision to reproduce them indeed, then. The Muldoon presumably rides on the back of *Horse Latitudes*; the Dunn, of what? Is it the case that Faber feel that the eminence of the editors demands re-publication ("Paul Muldoon is widely regarded as the leading Irish poet of his generation", as the blurb on *Irish* says); or does the presumed brilliance of each anthology itself seem to warrant its reappearance in this original form (poor Dunn receives no plaudits for his poetry on his cover, which raves instead that "Dunn's long introduction is exemplary")? In neither case does this argument seem entirely persuasive.

Muldoon, on the evidence of his new collection of poetry, continues profitably and humanely to play fast and loose with issues of history and belonging in his now well-established modes. The reappearance of this anthology, with its notorious inclusion as Preface of a discussion between F.R. Higgins and Louis MacNeice about poetry as "blood-music" versus poetry as "record of anything", is an interesting reminder that the provenance of Muldoon's truest poetry has always been in proximity to Ireland's various troubles. Yet such issues seem increasingly remote from the zippy free-wheeling allusiveness (and perhaps over-comfortable remoteness) of Muldoon's post-*Madoc* persona. The final selection from Heaney included here is the part of *Station Island* recounting, in terza rima, the murder of a local chemist. Remember the mock-shock of Muldoon's own lines about 'Doctor Heaney' from *The Prince of the Quotidian* (1994), that "the great physician of the earth / is waxing metaphysical", and marvel at the pure change that has happened in Irish poetry with the alteration of conditions on the ground, a change sadly not included here.

Dunn's acute and forensic delineation of the linguistic impulses within Scottish poetry in his Introduction, the decisions to be taken between (if it were possible) working in Gaelic, Scots, or a dialect-inflected English, remains of obvious pertinence, as does his challenging of T.S. Eliot's noxious question 'Was there a Scottish Literature?' Yet, from this perspective in time, his decision to devote so much of his remarks to the crabby brilliance of Hugh MacDiarmid, as a kind of precursor to all subsequent Scottish poetry, seems more dubious. MacDiarmid's poetry receives the most pages in the book; now, the poetry of Edwin Muir (which I suspect that Dunn all along prefers), a poetry open to, and deeply shadowed by, middle-European trauma and drabness, seems more immediate and pertinent. The recent publication of the *New Collected Poems* of W.S. Graham (yes, available from Faber) offers further confirmation of the other ways in which some Scottish work managed both to accommodate itself to the demands of modernism whilst firmly standing its own ground, able to see English from an outside perspective as just (and lovingly so) 'language'.

The predominant note of the poems gathered by Dunn in this anthology remains that of a bleak pastoral and is (it seems now) a bit folksy; a note which ratifies his assertion, in some sense, that Scottish poetry has arisen from harsher backgrounds than English, whilst retaining a greater closeness to its potential audience. It is, however, with a kind of relief that we turn now here to Robert Garioch's Edinburgh tales, or, more especially, to Edwin Morgan's 'Glasgow Sonnets', seemingly spitting defiance at that organicist notion of poetry and community which Dunn seems rather sentimentally eager to hold onto: "Blackhill and Govan, better sticks and stanes / should break your banes, for poets' words are ill / to hurt ye."

Aspects of both anthologies remain serviceable. One excitement of Muldoon's book when it first appeared was its integration of the work of Thomas Kinsella and John Montague into a broader dynamic of Irish poetry, and its presentation of them to a wider, British and American, audience. His selections from them, as from Kavanagh and MacNeice, remain exemplary. Dunn's brief selection from MacDiarmid is similarly representative, even if his extracts from the careers of MacCaig, Crichton Smith and Mackay Brown now seem somewhat less so. Other irritations remain in this particular reprint: the fact that some Scots words require glossing means that the poetry in the anthology is curiously offset towards the right of the page. Longer lines therefore have their final words 'dropped' off their ends to a space below. Dunn's decision to print only a few poems from most of his wide range of selected poets was frustrating on the volume's first appearance, and remains so; poignant is the fact that several of those newer and younger names amongst the chosen in 1992 no longer have any presence at all on the current poetry scene. If that is merely poignant, absolutely and unbearably depressing is that – such is Faber's editorial negligence with these volumes – many of those dead since the volume's first appearance seemingly live on in Dunn's Contents page, with no necessary 'd.' to follow their 'b.'.

Steven Matthews's latest book is *Modernism*, in the Arnold Context Series of which he is General Editor.

Liverpool Panopticon

TODD SWIFT

Paul Farley, *Tramp In Flames*, Picador, £8.99, ISBN 0330440071

Paul Farley's third collection is a panoptical survey of the ways in which various surveillance technologies (such as the speed camera) meet the British; in the process it writes a new kind of Nature poetry – one that is slightly denatured. *Tramp In Flames* is further haunted by themes of liquidity; and then again of "seeing things". Here the reflection is not from a narcissist's gaze into some pool, but is cast over his shoulder by a watcher – or watchers: poets and cultural references that add value and meaning to a difficult world. This richly doubled take on things is both troubling and somehow comforting. We are not alone. Vision brings light as well as the dark.

There's a long tradition, of course, of grounding visionary experience in terms related to encountering the spirit world, the informing dead; notably from Dante, via Heaney, to some of the last poems that great American poet, the late Michael Donaghy, wrote. It is therefore no wonder that Heaney's *Seeing Things* and Donaghy's way with a glass, darkly, echo through the best work of Farley's here, as in 'Requiem For A Friend':

> Slip in to the light. See if I'm afraid
> to look you in the face. When the dead return
> they've every right to step out from the shadows
> and harden once more in our field of vision.

Tramp In Flames is to be admired for this accomplished balancing of subjects and influences that create an interlaced pattern of rhyming images and concepts from start to finish. Farley drives across a variety of formal assays, establishing his rhythmic and tonal virtuosity, so, we get a haiku series, sonnets, a pantoum, complex longer poems, even a not entirely gripping prose poem at the end.

The theme of looking seems the best way in to the heart of the collection; its strongest and most moving half being the first, with the very good poems 'The Lapse', prize-winning 'Liverpool Disappears for a Billionth of a Second', 'The Newsagent' and 'Civic'. 'The Lapse', especially, connects ideas of cinema's construction of an imaginary world in the mind, with, potentially, a more romantic (even lost) one, deriving from poetry – as if Locke's empiricism and Shelley's "lifted veil" struggled for epistemic supremacy in language, in perception.

Here again, images of the visual and the liquid are coyly married, gently echoing Muldoon's poem 'The Boundary Commission' from *Why Brownlee Left*, where rain stops and becomes solid glass: "like a man who comes in bone dry from a downpour / by stopping the world and snapping out a path / through glassy rods right up to his front door."

A key to the whole book (in 'Civic') may be another very Muldoonian protagonist – the "private eye in *Chinatown*, hired / in a drought to find out what has happened to all the water" – where the themes of surveillance (and its never-too-far-away henchman violence) merge with pop culture (cinema) and an endangered environment (water, lost and found). Farley well knows *Chinatown* was Polanski's (and Towne's) own correlative for *The Waste Land*; and he locates his in the mediated images that gather concentrically once his imaginations breaks the surface of the reservoir on the outskirts of Manchester. When Farley archly observes that this "lake [is] a reservoir / disguised as a lake. It looks / the part alright; in fact, has already starred / in films as body double to Como and Geneva", he is mirroring sublime places that Romantic poets, and others, have loved in funhouse fashion (as in *Lady From Shanghai*).

Farley's 'looking' also traces aspects of 9/11 (indeed 7/7) paranoia in it; as if shadowed by a nightmarishly updated version of *The Conversation*. Consider these words and phrases from just the first six poems: "a full pan" ('The Front'); "until-now-never-before-seen footage" ('Night Swim'); "a plane being bowed across the sky" ('The Lapse'); "home from the optician" ('Ruin'); "the blink inside a blink" ('Liverpool Disappears for a Billionth of A Second'); "the first to see the snow" and "strikes and wars" ('The Newsagent'). Later, we find an "audiophilic" farmer (in some strange hybrid of Watergate and Descartes) bugging his scarecrow, then settling down in front of a fire to listen to his field, woken into nightmare when his own "Frankenstein boots" plod back to yank the listening device away. That's echoed, in turn, by 'The Big Hum' with its "baffled mic" and muffled echoes of Edward Thomas at the end "of Oxfordshire and Gloucestershire I hardly knew".

Farley posits a twenty-first century lyric mode where the poet no longer gets easy access to the real thing – whatever that may be – at the heart of nature's rolling sublime. Instead all is surface and curve; what radar can catch before the vehicle, if not the tenor, speeds away. *Tramp in Flames* represents one way in which mainstream twenty-first century poetry is likely to develop: as it marries thought and form with humour and feeling, with one haunted eye looking back, the other, curiouser, looking ahead.

Todd Swift is Oxfam poet-in-residence and the author of three collections of poetry.

A Scottish Polymath

PATRICK MCGUINNESS

W. N. Herbert, *Bad Shaman Blues*, Bloodaxe, £8.95, ISBN 1852247282

W. N. Herbert's poetic prescription is kill or cure. Herbert specialises in big, spine-burstingly various and formally eclectic books, in both Scots and English, that are always in the end unified by the energy, wit and intellectual adventurousness of their author. *Bad Shaman Blues* is no exception and, weighing in at 160 pages, it might be better thought of as several books in one by a writer who should by rights count as several poets in one.

In *Bad Shaman Blues* we move from Newcastle suburbs, such as Heaton and Jesmond, to Novosibirsk or Moscow by way of Sofia, Dumfries and Edinburgh. The book focuses on apparently marginal places and intermediary zones, visited by marginal and intermediary poetic figures. In one poem, shamanistic progress is imagined as a flight in a creaking Siberian plane, and the book is full of displaced artist figures. Here are Schwittters in Ambleside and Zamyatin in Heaton; and walk-on parts by Dostoevsky, Mandelstam and the irrepressible McGonagall, to whom Herbert pays a superb mock-homage in 'The Bridge Across the Rover Ob', in which, out of McGonagalesque necessity and on a one-time-only basis, Novosibirsk rhymes with Thirsk.

Bad Shaman Blues is also concerned with borders and frontiers; what they mean and symbolise, how they are crossed or how enforced. For a Scot living in Newcastle, the logical place to start is Hadrian's Wall. But because this is W. N. Herbert, the Great Wall of China comes soon after. Borders and frontiers make for fertile poetic tropes, but Herbert never descends into the standard paradoxes. 'Over the Wall' opens:

> True Wall, magnetic Wall,
> Wall that never mentions North
> But hints obliquely like an only line:
> Here begins beyond.

Later in the same poem he writes of the wall as a mirror that one passes through rather than a border that one crosses. This idea, a compelling one, is something the book revisits and plays variations on. These themes – otherness and self, walls and mirrors, travel and return – all hold this various collection together, and help to give it, beneath the humour and exuberance (there are some good jokes about Picts and the particular kind of obsessive self-differentiation that border-dwellers indulge in), a political dimension that is rarely far from the surface of Herbert's poetry. One aspect of this is his often-critical interest in the political possibilities of post-devolution Scotland, explored here in poems such as 'Rabotnik Fergusson'.

There are great expansive narrative poems about place and displacement, about poetry's marginalised status and the poet's post- or sub-Baudelairean irrelevance. But there are also shorter, sparer and more compressed lyrics, as impressive in their way. It is easy to overlook, in the rush of allusion and wit of the longer poems, Herbert's capacity for clear and often thrillingly exact images. This is 'Sideling Hieroglyphs':

> The hawk that shears the hedge, then steadies, held
> above the verge by urgent need, he is
> old Egypt's silhouette, the pictogram
> for 'Kill'. There is a lock to which he is
> continually the key that must release
> a narrow death from everywhere in air.
> He is the tender axe that has to fall.

W. N. Herbert uses poetry as a place to think in, to try things on and test things out. Like Edwin Morgan, another Scottish poetic polymath, Herbert is interested not in producing static verbal objects but in making a poetry that touches life in the greatest number of places. This is what makes his work seem, on the one hand, precariously experimental, and, on the other, already wholly achieved.

Patrick McGuinness's *The Canals of Mars* appeared from Carcanet in 2004.

☙

Here Is The News

PAUL BATCHELOR

Lorna Goodison, *Goldengrove: New and Selected Poems*, Carcanet, £9.95,
ISBN 1857548485; Philip Levine, *Stranger to Nothing: Selected Poems*,
Bloodaxe, £9.95, ISBN 1852247371; Dunya Mikhail, *The War Works Hard*,
Carcanet, £9.95, ISBN 1857548698

Here are three poets who differ greatly in their backgrounds,
resources and priorities; but are united by having had to create or
re-imagine their literary traditions. Lorna Goodison, for example,
was born and grew up in Jamaica, but now teaches at Michigan University.
She wonders about the effect of Western culture on her work: "Perhaps if
you remain you will become civilized, / detached, refined, your words
pruned of lush". I don't think there's any danger of this happening:
Goodison's language draws much of its strength from the divisions and
oppositions of Jamaica's history. To take just one example, when she refers to
the emancipation of chattel slavery as "1838 the year of general full free", we
sense the tension between the European imposition of the date and the
Anglo-Caribbean term for the event.

Perhaps such contradictions are necessary to a poet's development:
certainly, Goodison's twin virtues are her restraint and her ear for
incantatory rolling rhythm. Take these lines from 'Where the Flora of Our
Village Came From':

> Coffee, kola, ackee, yams, okra, plantain, guinea grass,
> tamarind seeds and herbs of language to flavor English;
> those germinated under our tongues and were cultured
> within our intestines during the time of forced crossings.

Here, Goodison characteristically matches delight in her language's
overflowing exuberance with exactitude and precision: consider the amount
of work being done by that deferred verb "cultured".

In 'So Who Was the Mother of Jamaican Art', Goodison describes a
"nameless woman" whose children have been sold into slavery. The woman
makes dolls as substitute children: "She suspended those wood babies from
a rope / round her neck, before she ate she fed them, / touched bits of
pounded yam and plantains / to sealed lips; always urged them to sip water."
The poem ends by telling us "She did not sign her work". The refusal to

expand on the event that triggered this compulsive behaviour – or to spell out the links the title makes between such anonymous acts of reparation and Jamaican culture – acts as a demand that the reader consider such issues. But I am in danger of making Goodison's work sound worthy, dry or dull. In fact, the fluency of her rhythms, the dazzling imagery and the celebratory impulse all make *Goldengrove* a distinguished, outstanding pleasure.

Since *On the Edge* in 1963, Philip Levine has produced a new book of poems every two or three years. His work ethic is unsurprising: a chronicler of industrial life in Detroit, Levine writes poetry "for people for whom there is no poetry." This might make Levine sound like a counterpart for Fred Voss, but the differences are significant: Levine has greater emotional range and has stayed more open, more vulnerable and more melancholy than his compatriot (though there is humour, too: see 'Gin' or 'A Theory of Prosody'). In Levine's world, the threat of premature death by industrial accident, violence, alcohol or the army is never far away. Even more prevalent is an insidious death-in-life; a mostly-unspoken sense of defeat that haunts poems like 'Starlight,' in which the poet remembers, aged four, being asked by his father if he is happy. His father's voice is "somehow thick and choked, / a voice I have not heard before, but / heard often since".

Knowing he is one of the lucky ones, Levine has all the knotty feelings of a survivor. In 'The Escape' he writes: "O Lord of Life, / how much you made them pay so I could love". For this reason, there is a distinct sense of the transcendent moments in his poetry having been earned and paid for: they are never easily escapist. 'The Simple Truth' begins: "I bought a dollar and a half's worth of small red potatoes, / took them home, boiled them in their jackets / and ate them for dinner with a little butter and salt." The poem ends:

> Can you taste
> what I'm saying? It is onions or potatoes, a pinch
> of simple salt, the wealth of melting butter, it is obvious,
> it stays in the back of your throat like a truth
> you never uttered because the time was always wrong,
> it stays there for the rest of your life, unspoken,
> made of the dirt we call earth, the metal we call salt,
> in a form we have no words for, and you live on it.

I strongly recommend this outstanding book.

Dunya Mikhail is an Iraqi poet currently living in the United States. Her most recent poems are found in the first and longest section of *The War Works Hard*. Although Saadi Simawe's introduction describes these poems as child-like (albeit like the wise, subversive child of The Emperor's New Clothes), these are songs of experience rather than innocence. When the truth is as bitter and bleak as this, it requires irony if it is to be expressed at all. This is from 'Bag of Bones':

> What good luck!
> She has found his bones.
> The skull is also in the bag
> the bag in her hand
> like all other bags
> in all other trembling hands.
> His bones, like thousands of bones
> in the mass graveyard […]

In the brilliant title poem, Mikhail displays a Brechtian knack for finding the unexpected angle that can illuminate a situation afresh. The poem begins "How magnificent the war is!" and goes on to form an ironic hymn of praise to war:

> It inspires tyrants
> to deliver long speeches,
> awards medals to generals
> and themes to poets.
> It contributes to the industry
> of artificial limbs,
> provides food for flies,
> adds pages to the history books […]

The War Works Hard closes with poems written in Baghdad during the Iran-Iraq war. These pieces are more demanding, with the irony working as a necessary encrypting device for the author's sympathies (see the gnomic 'Nun'). The bulk of the book is taken up with the later, more public poetry in which Mikhail finds ways of writing about Iraq without indulging in sloganeering, glibness, cynicism or any of the other prefabrications commentators use to avoid the truth. In Elizabeth Winslow's clear, unfussy translation, an important new voice in world poetry can be heard in English.

Paul Batchelor's *To Photograph a Snow Crystal* is reviewed on pp. 98–100.

Raising The Bar

MICHAEL HULSE

Justin Quinn, *Waves and Trees*, Gallery Press, £8.50, ISBN 1852354003;
Andrew McNeillie, *Slower*, Carcanet, £9.95, ISBN 1857548280;
Paul Batchelor, *To Photograph a Snow Crystal*,
Smith/Doorstop Books, £3, ISBN 190238282X;
Andrew Greig, *This Life, This Life. New & Selected Poems* 1970-2006,
Bloodaxe, £10.95, ISBN 1852247134

They might be the line-up for an old-style groan-inducing joke, this gang of four: an Englishman, an Irishman, a Welshman and a Scot. The mercy is that, excepting McNeillie (the Welshman), they don't go on about national matters. For this relief much thanks.

Justin Quinn is that familiar phenomenon, the Irishman abroad in Central Europe. No European city worth its salt lacks for an Irish pub, and the Irish by now have a substantial modern tradition (at least as old as Joyce and Beckett) of embracing the welcome that Europe extends. Quinn pays handsome tribute to his adopted home, Prague, in the sequence of twenty sonnets that's at the centre of this fourth collection. One of the sonnets versifies words by the great 19th century Czech writer Jan Neruda (from whom Chile's Pablo adopted his surname in homage); another recounts the familiar labours of Mozart to write *Don Giovanni* (which was premiered in Prague); another returns to that great General of the Thirty Years' War, Wallenstein, to whom Schiller devoted a sublime stage trilogy (if I read him correctly, Quinn thinks Wallenstein was assassinated in Prague). In other words, over a decade after entering the employ of the Charles University, and with a Czech wife, Justin Quinn has a proper sense of the substance of this fine city, and broaches it in a polished, urbane manner that owes something to Brodsky (but is happily free of the Russian's imperiousness).

Elsewhere in the book (and hence its title) there are poems that record a fact that sooner or later hits every islander with an almost primaeval force: continental Europe is still a great tract of immense forests and rivers. That fundamental understanding may be the backbone of Quinn's new book, but its great attraction as poetry lies in the blithe lyric gift that is the mainspring of the sixteen twelve-line poems in dimeter that close the volume. This is 'Tattoo':

> A swirl of colour
> up from her ass.

Philippe Sollers
says gods harass

the human race
because they love
not fanes and praise
of heavens above

but young girls naked.
Their flesh is lipped
by this first sacred
manuscript.

Something of a debt to the late Anthony Hecht (and perhaps also the Australian Geoff Page?) is glimpsed there, as is the density Quinn commands even at his seeming simplest. *Waves and Trees* is a marvellous collection, light in its touch, engaging in tone, and civilised in stance.

Andrew McNeillie shares Quinn's concern for a serious engagement with cultural substance, and he too has a weakness for the sonnet, but the two poets could scarcely be more different in tone. The sestet of one sonnet in an eleven-piece sequence that chats allusively about the poet's formative years runs like this:

My true Penelope (as the poet said)
wasn't Petrarch's Laura but Zhivago's
Julie Christie, and all the girls from head
to foot her look-alikes in maxi-coats, high boots
(I tell it like it was) and back-combed hairdos.
And all the mophead boys were poets?

That much is like a *Guardian Weekend* version of early Peter Porter. Elsewhere, in 'Meditation in a Private Garden', McNeillie's autumn is the moment when "gravity grasps the nettle itself / to bring everything down to earth"; and when he isn't engaged in wordplay he declares in Victorian vein, "Virtuous purpose has great merit". (What order of irony is at work here, if any?) In other words, he's working very efficiently, and to various ends, across a range of tones: where Quinn's lyricism is full-throated, McNeillie writes as the self-aware intellectual, forever qualifying his own utterance, reflecting, undercutting. It's almost a surprise to find one so adept in the ironies referring to poetry – in the thirteenth of his 'Glyn Dŵr Sonnets', a meditation on Welshness – as his "calling". But then again, it isn't; for

Andrew McNeillie pleases by having his cake and eating it, by staking his claim to the high Parnassian ground and, within lines, throttling back to a companionably marital demotic, apologising to his wife for being absent from bed in order to write verses, and comparing that absence with the much longer absences of Owain Glyn Dŵr from *his* wife:

> I would ask what was it like for her
> to be caught up in history? But then
> she wasn't, much, was she? Not so you'd hear.

Ovid, perhaps too often invoked as the hero of recent poetry, appears "with his one-way ticket" in McNeillie, and moves centre-stage in Paul Batchelor's accomplished pamphlet. "Winter is cruel. / I think continually of my last night in Rome. / Wolves move nimbly on the ice to bring down deer." That much, from 'Tristia', might as well have come from the Ovid novels of a David Malouf or Christoph Ransmayr. Turn the page, and 'Keening' borrows registers from sources as different as Shakespeare and Pound's usury canto. Throughout, there are too many reminders of other writers' tones – but that is the full extent of my reservations. The fact is that Batchelor has an imagination and possesses resources of form, information and vocabulary, and he's not afraid to use any of them. 'The Permafrost: an A–Z' is comparable to Penelope Shuttle's 'Poem' (in *Redgrove's Wife*) or early John Ash, and suggests just why everyone is so glad of Paul Batchelor's arrival on the scene:

> The Permafrost sounds like an ailing synthesiser. It is 1982 at
> the best of times. "They used to grow grapes here," the natives
> boast. How little must have been promised these people; how
> little they must feel they are owed: they do not even refer to
> their ancestors as 'we'.

Finally, Andrew Greig's hefty volume adds sixteen new poems ("a late infestation of recent poems", according to the author's note) to a selection of his work from seven books, the latest published in 2001. They have his characteristic air of talking his way through the lines, brushing up against the dull and the wonderful and never troubling too much (in the ways that Quinn, McNeillie and Batchelor do) about raising the bar and trying for something that little bit harder.

Michael Hulse's *Empires and Holy Lands. Poems 1976-2000* was published by Salt in 2002.

Michael Longley
The Holly Bush

in memory of Dorothy Molloy

Frosty Carrigskeewaun. I am breaking ice
Along the salt marsh's soggy margins
And scaring fieldfares out of the holly bush
And redwings, their consorts, chestnut-brown
Flashing one way, chestnut-red another,
Fragments of the January dawn-light
That Killary focuses on the islands
Before it clears the shoulder of Mweelrea.
Caher Island and Inishturk are frosty too.
In the short-lived spotlight they look like cut-
Outs and radiate apricot from within.
I learn of your death in this weather and
Of your book arriving the day after,
Your first and last slim volume. Dorothy,
You read your poems just once and I was there.
The poets you loved are your consorts now.
A hundred or more golden plovers turn
And give back dawn-light from their undersides.
The edge of the dunes wears a fiery fringe.

Ruthlessly Edited

PATRICK CROTTY

Seán Dunne, *Collected Poems*, Ed. Peter Fallon,
Gallery, £9.95, ISBN 1852353945;
Dorothy Molloy, *Gethsemane Day*, Faber, £8.99, ISBN 057122976X

Death is the most ruthless of all editors, calling in copy at a non-negotiable deadline like an invigilator at the end of an examination. Is the poet who hears the minutes counted down more or less fortunate than the one who sits all unsuspecting as the invigilator swoops to take away his/her papers? Dorothy Molloy knew she was running out of time, and many of the poems in *Gethsemane Day* vividly attest to the power of mortal illness to estrange us from ourselves and from the world. Seán Dunne died suddenly of a heart attack, his poetry stopping short just as it was winning to distinctiveness after twenty years of unrelenting effort. Molloy is much the more considerable poet, but she had almost a quarter of a century longer to hone her art than Dunne, and was unknown to the world before the appearance of *Hare Soup* in the month of her death at sixty-two in 2004. The career constituted by her two emphatically slim volumes seems all the more dazzling for being over as soon as it began. Dunne's *Collected* is less the record of a career than of the apprenticeship for one: the book is a touching monument to the intensity, persistence and ultimately the seriousness of his desire to achieve poetry.

The poems of Dunne's *Against the Storm* (1985) can be gauche servants of that desire, forcing their materials into an empty plangency. 'The Fifth Beatle', frequently anthologised in Ireland, provides a painful instance of the attempted shortcut to frisson. Millions of Beatles fans have for decades been familiar with the story of Stuart Sutcliffe, and the poem's conceit that they want to deny his existence as some Germans want to deny the reality of Nazi extermination camps is groundless. The fans, alas, know rather more about Sutcliffe than Dunne did – they know he turned his back on stage to hide his inept bass playing, they know he had left the group before his death, they know he was a gifted painter rather than a musician. They know enough, that is to say, to recognise the double falsity of the poem's climactic observation that Sutcliffe "made no more than music". Personal subject matter, also, tends to be over-egged by Dunne, typically in the direction of a domestic idyll of warm interiors, hand-woven fabrics and health foods. The tonal procedures of these poems are recognisably those of some of the most prominent of the senior Irish poets of the 1980s: Dunne strives for the stanzaic elegance of Derek Mahon and the moralising voice-over of John Montague but lacks the insouciant resourcefulness of the one and the (sometimes saving) grace of the other.

The Sheltered Nest (1992) is a firmer book, less betrayed by ambition beyond its means, though Dunne's language can still be dismayingly inaccurate (the opening of 'Throwing the Beads', for example, invites us to imagine and emigrant simultaneously "setting out from North Kerry" and taking off from Shannon Airport in County Clare). There is writing of real quality in 'Sydney Place', where the poet quietly mourns the collapse of his marriage by way of a series of sharply observed vignettes of the once genteel apartment in which it was conducted. Low-key, attentive and non-assertive, 'Sydney Place' anticipates the delicate imagism of 'Letter to Lisbon', 'Still Lives' and the handful of other pieces that make *Time and the Island* (1996), despatched to the publisher a fortnight before his death, much the strongest of Dunne's individual collections. Three other poems from 1995 reproduced here for the first time suggest that he was heading for high marks when the invigilator intervened.

Dorothy Molloy's poems plump onto the page without glosses: their power resides partly in their brazen outstaring of the reader, their simultaneous Come On and Fuck Off to interpretation. Thus 'Barbie' works on one level as a feminist lyric with a predictable politics of representation, on another as a baffling, un-visualisable narrative about a doll made out of plasticine, rotten eggs and papier-mâché. 'Grief Therapy' appears to relish the self-destructive violence of its mastectomied anti-heroine, a domestic cat. Are the heavy internal rhymes meant to comment on attempts by earlier poets to replicate the assonantal patterning of Gaelic verse, and perhaps even to conjure the shade of Pangur Bán, Irish poetry's iconic cat? There is no way of telling. The contents of *Gethsemane Day* are brutal, colourful, full of bounce and surprise – and almost impossible to generalise about. 'Philomena McGillicuddy Becomes Unstuck', for instance, is clearly an allegory, an outrageous one of the collapse of ecclesiastical authority in Ireland. 'Trophy' brings machismo, violence and (arguably) menstruation together in a vibrant, repulsive cartoon. 'Last Night the Itch' meditates on rectal discomfort (MacDiarmid's Drunk Man describes consciousness as "a rumplefyke in Heaven's doup" but otherwise the modern poetry of these islands, so far as I am aware, remains silent on the topic of anal itching). The no-go subject of sexual abuse of a young girl by a man is brilliantly, shockingly, commentlessly rendered in 'Ghost Train', a kind of anti-sonnet. Another fourteen-liner, 'Deansgrange', extracts a spooky intensity from its repetition of the broken English phrase 'Please to Remember' in relation to a succession of relatives who have beaten the speaker to the cemetery.

Gethsemane Day gives no indication as to what proportion of its contents was written before the diagnosis of the author's apparently brief final illness. The last eleven poems in the book, at any rate, offer a frightening commentary on the course of Molloy's hospital treatment. The wide-eyed, plonkety-plonk rhythms of the title-piece pitilessly stress the grimness of their subject matter:

> What cocktail is Daddy preparing for me?
> What ferments in pathology's sink?
> Tonight they will tell me, will proffer the cup,
> and like it or not, I must drink.

Much of the force of this comes from the contrast between the two modalities of comparison: the little girl taking her medicine, the agony of Christ in the Garden. Some of these deathbed poems are extremely plain in diction and approach, while others are as inventive in conception and rhetoric as anything in the author's tiny *oeuvre*. 'Mid-Winter', a steady, hopeless, post-Christian *Nocturnall Upon St Lucies Day*, is notable among the more direct poems, while 'Freed Spirit' and 'Life Boat' provide perhaps the most striking late examples of the extravagant, ludic side of Molloy's poetic personality. The first of these offers an appropriately dizzying patient's-eye-view of a CAT Scan, while the second pictures the skull of the dying speaker as her own ship of death. Opulently figurative, 'Life Boat' can be read as resigned, ironic or angry. Perhaps I may be permitted to end this brief account of a remarkable book with lines that show Dorothy Molloy sailing into our imaginations as she sails out to her reward:

> And lo, God's gifts
> lay scattered
> all about: rare Paracletes with tongues of fire;
>
> and Englishman with ropes and gamp; a singing bird, an olive branch,
> a box of nard,
> a spirit-lamp, safe passage to the cedar-groves of Lebanon.

Patrick Crotty is Professor of Irish and Scottish Literature at the University of Aberdeen. He is editor of the forthcoming *New Penguin Book of Irish Verse*.

☙

Love's Body

GRAHAM HARTILL

Frances Presley, *Myne, New & Selected Poems & Prose 1976-2005*,
Shearsman, £11.95, ISBN 0907562876;
Gael Turnbull, *There Are Words, Collected Poems*,
Shearsman, £18.95, ISBN 0907562894;
Elaine Randell, *Selected Poems, 1970-2005*,
Shearsman, £9.95, ISBN 090756271X

Frances Presley has opened my eyes anew to the place of the poet in landscape. Her technique is kind and meticulous; reminding me of drawing, or the super-sensitive processes of archaeology with brushes. The perception, discovery and reclamation of occasions is indistinguishable here from the actual *work* of, and within, language.

In an article, 'Common Pink Metaphor: from The Landscape Room to Somerset Letters', she writes: "For a long time my experience of the countryside in the twentieth century was a place of diminishing relevance, and dying communities. I want to explore how and why my attitude towards the country has changed and how that change also takes place in my writing practice". This is not poetry of place in any conventional sense, but more like poetry *as* place: an act of resistance against the colonisation of our language, the alienation of our desires.

After a recent reading in Abergavenny, a friend of mine previously unfamiliar with Presley's work said that, while it's usual to expect a poem to turn within itself, maybe stanza by stanza or line by line, what's different here is the turn *within a word*. Presley footnotes one of the poems included here, 'Culbone': "I was writing in the half-light, allowing language to form and reform." This is the kind of reading, too, the work requires.

In the opening poem of the title sequence, addressed to the poet Tilla Brading, Presley writes:

> Tilla, the tides
> the tides
> are always too early
> or too late
> to swallow
> words
> nowhere to lay them
> on the beach

crests cannot

catch up

too many, white, commas

clustering

not spacing

Not just form-equals-content, or the postmodern poet's obsession with writing as subject, this is an apprehension of physical space; the space of images or of relationship turning even a comma. The title *Myne* is a pun of course (better to use a word which the poet is fond of, "wordplay"). 'Myne' has Celtic origins – it means the top of the hill – but Presley doesn't want to mythologize a patriarchal warrior tribe, preferring to dwell (her family were miners) on an ironic play on the word 'mine' in a kind of playground layout. Open field means open page-space, opening meaning. "I try," she writes, "to dislocate the sense of the individual's lyric eye." Such techniques include passages where, she says, "There are painful angles, not smoothed over by grammar." Painful? Well, only for readers unprepared for a challenge to their assumptions about what poetry is. Approach Presley's poetry with an eye for painting, say (she works a lot with visual artists), and you won't have the problem of pain. People wanting to open up their reading couldn't do better than to investigate this volume. Due to the integrity of Presley's intricate process, it feels like several books in one: the poems keep opening, opening out, the more you read them. This is a book in which we are more than commonly included.

Gael Turnbull is a major figure in modern English writing. Born in Scotland, brought up in Canada and the USA and practising on both sides of the Atlantic as a doctor, his role in bringing American modernist poetry to British attention – and thereby encouraging home-grown experimentation – was considerable. Strongly influenced by objectivism, Turnbull loved the clarity and concreteness of the finished object, much of his work appealing to those who are drawn to the art of, say, Ian Hamilton Finlay; or the terseness of haiku. But there is rich stuff here too; the emotional dirt, as it were, left dangling on the roots. At his death in 2004 he left a considerable body of writing that reads like a map of the "other" poetry since the war, characterised by a joyful openness of form and wide range of content.

No quotation from the book can sum it up, it's so diverse, so wide. Let's leave it at this: that this beautiful Shearsman production is essential (and I use the word advisedly) to everyone engaged with the broader possibilities of poetry. To paraphrase Roy Fisher: "Of all our lost friends, he is the least dead":

Not the degredations
of a metronome

or the mere contriving
of better mousetraps

but an architecture of
pauses

and evidence
like a footprint.

('If He Sings It')

Elaine Randell has a reputation for her work, poetic and social, with what are now known as dysfunctional families. The poems that deal directly with her encounters with the socially and emotionally deprived are compassionate and intense, often gathering power from the language of testimony, of uncompromised observation and quotation:

His mother, a petrol pump attendant, was said by those who knew her to be less than bright[...]. On the forecourt of the garage she went into labour while delivering three gallons of four star. They stifled her screams with the rag that wiped the dip stick and mopped her waters with the sponge that cleaned the windscreens.

('Hard to Place')

But it would be a mistake to buttonhole Randell's work as 'social work poetry'. Having read her books in the 80s (not much has been published since), I was knocked out by seeing it gathered together; realizing again that here we have some very important artistry indeed. The depth of her language folds inside the experiences she writes about, whether of self or others; and it is always felt in the heart. Here is strength, even toughness, of mind at the service of our humanity, at the truth of life as it is lived in our country today. It is never less than a poetry of the body, specifically the woman's body, presented at work, in the sauna, in childbirth, shopping; bruised, chapped, standing straight in spite of it all. And the poems themselves refuse easy technical options. They are physical but inventive; we can have no casual encounter with them, we can't pass them by with a nod of the head; we are *involved* with them:

> The worn warm ways of the world
> weary with repetition
> it is the only form of permanence
> that we see.
> Our learning
> does not come only from our sorrows
> look how common is our blood.

('Men Must Live And Create. Live To The Point Of Tears.')

It is a shame that Randell's work is not routinely regarded amongst the very finest being produced in Britain. Shearsman Books are to be complemented on doing sterling work on our behalf.

Graham Hartill's latest book is *Cennau's Bell: Poems 1980-2001* (Collective Press, 2005).

ℬ

Three Welsh Poets

GILES GOODLAND

Owen Sheers, *Skirrid Hill*, Seren, £7.99, ISBN 1854114034;
Vernon Watkins, *New Selected Poems*, Carcanet, £9.95, ISBN 1857548477;
Dannie Abse, *Running Late*, Hutchinson, £9.99, ISBN 0091796970

Owen Sheers is in love with metaphor, and will pursue one to the death. He relies heavily on the poeticism, '[noun] of [noun]', in which 'of' relates a similitude. In the first poem in *Skirrid Hill*, 'Mametz Wood', Sheers has "A chit of bone, the china plate of a shoulder blade"; "broken bird's egg of a skull"; "a broken mosaic of bone" and more. These sound good, but are too much together; this is in a twenty-one-line poem that also includes a "like" and an "as if". Nor does he mind mixing metaphors with clunky personification, until you do not know where one starts and the other begins:

> even now the earth stands sentinel,
> reaching back into itself for reminders of what happened
> like a wound working a foreign body to the surface of the skin.

This is grand-sounding, but has many ill-matched layers of meaning. A "reminder" should be fresh, a way of seeing something anew. This poem just reminds me of other poems.

Perhaps the bone-in-a-field genre has gone on too long. Any writer coming to the subject now should say something more than that the dead have turned to bone, and look like different things. I enjoy excess in poetry if it is serving a purpose, but here it seems evasive, looking away from what things (particularly bones) are; as opposed to what they resemble. The beautiful-sounding language is carrying the subject, but it should be the other way round. After all, the best poets on that war, the ones who were actually there – David Jones fought at Mametz Wood – learnt through experience to avoid the easy poetic gestures of their time.

The problem with metaphors (and Sheers uses them with similar density throughout this book) is that as they accumulate, they lessen. In 'Night Windows' we have:

> you lowered yourself to me,
> the curves of a distant landscape

opening across your pelvis,
your body slicked and valleyed
in the August heat
and your back arching like a bow […]

There are not many bones in this poetry, once the rhetoric and metaphors are dug away. The front cover of the book describes Owen's work (quoting a review of his previous collection) as "confident, glittering, and suggestive". I would certainly agree with the confidence part. Glitters and suggestions are there too, like gaudy wrapping-paper over stale chocolates. The fact that Sheers knows how to sound good is a problem; his poems may find an appreciative audience, but will not suit anyone who likes to think as they read poetry.

The problem of sounding good was something Vernon Watkins wrestled with all his life, destroying the hundreds of poems he wrote before his first volume for fear that they were inauthentic. He later had the useful though doomed task of grounding Dylan Thomas. This *New Selected Poems* reminds us how much a quiet life dedicated to the craft of poetry, disregarding the extraneous, can achieve. Watkins knew that things are mostly what they are; and used metaphors seldom, but with intelligence. Here he is with his own bow-and-arrow metaphor:

> An image in the water shone below,
> Armed with a secret we could not deliver.
> Those beams were like the arrows in a quiver
> For which our expectation was the bow.
>
> ('Two Sources of Life')

The reader has to do some thinking here, but it pays off.

Watkins could also start a poem with the wonderful excess of "Late I return, O violent, colossal, reverberant, eavesdropping sea" ('Taliesin in Gower'), or, more usually, with the ballad-form that suited him so well:

> When I was born on Amman hill
> A dark bird crossed the sun.
> Sharp on the floor the shadows fell;
> I was the youngest sun.
>
> ('The Collier')

While reading these poems I was surprised to be reminded of early Basil Bunting. Imagine a Bunting who did not encounter Pound, and who stayed in the area where he was born. I think that Watkins was too static a writer to ever achieve the dialectical fusion of *Briggflatts*. He was a writer of moments and visions; his narratives are often unconvincing. But what incredible moments he could achieve, particularly the synaesthetic 'Music of Colours' poems. One small consideration: this book sells for £9.95. His *Collected* is currently on Amazon for £11.18. Currently, that is, until I buy it.

It is impressive to publish a collection of new poems in your mid-eighties. To maintain a freshness of style and inventiveness of subject, as Dannie Abse does in *Running Late*, is truly remarkable. Starting with an inscription from the 3rd-century Chinese of Han Fei, "It's easy to paint a ghost, damned difficult to paint a horse", his poems in fact contain as many unsentimental ghosts as difficult horses. Inevitably, there is a lot of looking back, with many departed friends to lament. He writes about death with a doctor's realism and matter-of-factness, not looking away. His view of life is quirky and cantankerous, as someone freed from the illusions of youth and middle-age. But what stands out above this is humour and humanity. I recommend this book: and not just to members of Abse's own generation.

Giles Goodland works as a lexicographer. His latest book is *Capital* (Salt, 2006).

ℬ

"Black And Deep Desires":
Killing Crows And Drinking Guinness

CHARLOTTE NEWMAN

Patrick Lane, *Syllable of Stone*, Arc, £8.99, ISBN1904614299;
Mutsuo Takahashi, *On Two Shores*, Dedalus, £8.20, ISBN 1904556493

Canadian poet Patrick Lane has just published his first British collection, with an almost hyperbolically admiring introduction by John Kinsella; and it is an unsettling affair. *Syllable of Stone* is set firmly in the bleak landscape of a Canada that is not "rural" but "early, industrial": a landscape in which violence is so commonplace as not to raise an eyebrow – or at least not to provoke discussion. Lane's is a reticent Canada; and his syllables indeed seem to be made of stone: hard, sharp and brutal when used in the right way.

Kinsella asserts in the introduction: "the intensity of Patrick Lane's poetry arises out of a tension and dislocation between the need to tell a story, and the need to step away from it". This could perhaps be refined further: Lane's poetics is indeed driven by narrative, but it is very often unflinching, unobstructed by self-imposed distance from reality, as Kinsella suggests. Lane puts this down to the mercilessness of his native surroundings:

> Because I never learned how
> to be gentle and the country
> I lived in was hard with dead
> animals and men, I didn't question
> my father when he told me
> to step on the kitten's head
> after the bus had run over
> its hind quarters.

Lane's narratives depict an insular environment and evoke a lonely atmosphere, couched in masculine, almost primal language. Animals are frequent characters, and their slaughter a frequent conclusion. But amid the tales of gutting blackbirds and nursing severed hands with irreverence, there are moments of more wistful contemplation. The collection is peppered with conditionals and speculative expressions: "maybe" and "perhaps". A case in point is 'There is a Time'. The speaker observes a scene in stasis, like a tableau, and desires desperately to frame a story around its characters and circumstances. Complicity is created with the reader, predicated on the assumption of an emotional engagement with all the scene's open ends:

> Maybe it is not the man she waits for.
> We want it to be someone. We want
> someone to relieve this hour.

Here the usually blinkered or blind-eye-turned perspective gives way to a sense of empathy; it is a rare moment in which the stony stoicism of the parochial male voice that underpins these poems becomes emotionally involved with its subject.

In *Syllable of Stone* there is also an element of concern with ontology. The sequence of 'Winter' poems considers the nature of life set against a world whitened and rendered innocent by snowfall, in which the poet's tone becomes questioning; sometimes with pessimism, sometimes with optimism, and sometimes with complete neutrality: "So many questions, / as in *what?* or *where?*" This musing on existence, more specifically on the concept of metaphysical beginnings and endings, is a trait that characterises the parallel-text collection from Japanese poet Mutsuo Takahashi, entitled *On Two Shores*. Indeed, many of the early poems in the collection appear less like poems and more like pseudo-philosophy with line breaks. Occasionally the perpetual stream of questions holds the reader's interest due to their sheer whimsicality, but at times Takahashi appears to tie himself in knots, and the reader's brain along with it:

> He will catch a reflection of rosy happiness
> or be eclipsed by violet despair.
> Light emitted
> from someone who doesn't exist
> to someone who didn't yet,
> and viewed by someone else again who doesn't yet exist,
> that is to say, light emitted from nothing to nothing [...]
> does any of it really exist?

Who knows – but the use of the word "violet" as a surprising adjective rather undermines itself here by the very fact that it is not surprising – it merely recalls *The Waste Land*. And herein lies the inescapable problem that tarnishes all literature written in a language foreign to the reader: we cannot know whether "violet" is the exact word that Takahashi wrote. This difficulty of the way in which the exact language has been filtered, and possibly partially lost, through translation, is of even more significance here, considering the pictographical nature of Japanese.

This is an Irish edition, a project that began its journey to fruition following a tour of Ireland that Takahashi made in 1999, which helped him "regain his faith in poetry". As such, the collection itself has another kind of duality – not merely linguistic but cultural. Two poems concern biological terrorist attacks in Japan; another broaches war and genocide in Japan, while many others are odes to Ireland and its literary heritage; not to mention its drinking habits. One poem, 'The Process', is dedicated to Michael Longley and Ciaran Carson, and reflects, not unfavourably, on the idea that, even on this faith-affirming poetry tour, poetry itself is merely a stepping stone to the pastime of drinking:

> And did the audience just play along,
> waiting patiently for the reading to end
> so we could all unwind up here with a drink?
> To say so doesn't take away from poetry.

For if my poems serve as a step up
to a higher place, they'll have done their bit.

This sense of humility as a poet, and Takahashi's easy acknowledgement of the importance of Guinness, goes some way to explaining how this Japanese poet has written so successfully about Ireland: he has assimilated the Irish culture, and reconsidered his role as a poet from an entirely different cultural background accordingly. *On Two Shores* is an engaging marriage of two literary traditions.

Charlotte Newman is at Selwyn College, Cambridge.

ℬ

The dedication of this poem is to A.G. because Assia Wevill's original name – and the name she used for her excellent Yehuda Amichai translations – was Guttman. 'The Yellow Plate' itself was, maybe still is, at Hawthornden Castle, where I stayed as one of the first 'fellows'. I was absolutely smitten by it and slowly deduced that it must depict the Chinese zodiac. The one useful reference book (because it was in the very early days, and the library shelves were still almost empty) was an old edition of the *Britannica*, and when I got back to London I saw that it had given me enough information for the poem. It was only as I kept looking at the plate, held it and made notes about all the figures on it, that I realised I was writing an elegy to Assia. The yellow colour of the rim was exactly the same yellow as some curtains of hers which Olwen Hughes gave me after Assia's death. The poem was first published in my collection *The Knot*, 1990. – R.F.

Ruth Fainlight
The Yellow Plate

i.m. A. G.

A painted plate, yellow-glazed below
the shallow curve of its white porcelain rim,
(yellow I'm always drawn to:
the saffron robe of a mendicant
> or the silk curtains a friend bought in Burma,
> mine now, because she's dead),
is the yellow road of the sun –
that bright furrow ploughed between the stars.

Underneath is the painter's complex square mark,
lacquer red, and round scarlet stickers reading:
'Chia ching' 'and 1796 to
1820'. On the front, twelve creatures.

It took a long time to see
they were the Chinese zodiac,
animal, bird, and reptile, real
or imagined (the one in the centre
is a dragon, not a crocodile),
that give names to the hours of the day
and the little twelve-day cycle,
the months of the year and the sixty years
I guess was the expected life span
of those hunters and shepherds.
       When she died, my friend was younger.

Tradition has it that Tajao, a minister
of Emperor Hwang-ti, circa
2697 B.C., invented them.
So little has changed since, the same
names are still used, (though I can't compute
what our year is by that calendar,
nor my own sign), and I sensed before
I knew what they meant and were.

The colours are green and red and yellow –
jade, cinnabar and sulphur,
the drawn line blackish sepia.
A pale wash of pink fills
the bodies of the wrinkle-snouted pig
and the rat, whose ideograph is 'water'.
Too anxious for the luxury
of variation the rabbit is pure white.

Cloudy patterns blotch the horse,
whose mane and tail fall fine and soft
as new-washed hair, and the bristling dog,
like shadow dappling windblown corn.
Flamy stripes unite the horned sheep and
the thoughtful tiger biting a raised paw.
Dragon and serpent are scaled, chequered
and barred, their dangerous twirling tongues
high-voltage warnings.

The hen looks fierce as a cock, crested
and hook-clawed, not domestic
and submissive like the ox
with a rope through its round nostril.
The monkey has delicate hands, subtle
lips and watchful eyes – a courtier
wondering if he's telling the right story.

Everything about the plate – all
the moods and colours, characters and patterns –
     she was like all of it,
     as beautiful.

❧

Yehuda Koren and Eilat Negev, *A Lover of Unreason: the Life and Tragic Death of Assia Wevill* Robson Books, hb £20, ISBN 1861059744

If a great biography weds scholarly rigour with an eloquent writing style, then *A Lover of Unreason* is not a great biography. It is, however, a compassionate account of a woman made famous for her affair with Ted Hughes and, sadly, for taking her life and that of their child. The authors worked over fifteen years on this book, speaking with those closest to Assia including Hughes; it was the only personal interview he ever granted. Magnetic, beautiful and cultured, by the time she was in her thirties Assia Wevill had lived around the world, been thrice divorced and was a 'career woman': to this extent openly defying conventions. Her translations of Yehuda Amichai were well-received. But this is not what draws us to her. Rather, it is our desire (or morbid curiosity?) to hear the mistress speak that turns the pages. And though Hughes is portrayed as a tortured philanderer, her biography holds its greatest interest for his fans, providing instead an opportunity to finally meet the "many blooded beauty" with "her tiger painted nails".

Margaux Poueymirou is a doctoral student at the University of St Andrews.

ENDPAPERS

Ah, the biog – a thing of ugly beauty.
—Lemn Sissay

LETTER FROM TAVISTOCK PLACE

CHRIS HOLIFIELD

For many poets it is a matter of real distress that so much of their work is out of print. Many readers feel mystified that important work is not available and cannot understand why publishers do not reprint it. For the Poetry Book Society, that was the starting-point of our *Back in Print* programme, the first six titles in which are available shortly and formally published in January. Our brief is to focus on the latest poetry, right down to a specific concentration for our Selectors on what is coming out that quarter. But, looking at the work of contemporary poets, it seemed clear that we should also promote recent work which has already seen the light of day but then vanished out of sight again.

Something important is lost if a collection is never to be seen again in its original form, but cherry-picked to produce a *Selected* (really a 'best of' under another name), where the poet and editor always have to make compromises regarding what goes in and what does not. In effect what has so often disappeared is the significance of the collection itself, the way the poet has compiled and arranged the poems in it, and the relationship between them.

The PBS is a small organisation and most of our time is taken up with running the day-to-day submission processes, producing the *Bulletin* and supplying books to our members. The Next Generation Poets promotion stretched us to our limits and our online bookshop www.poetrybookshoponline.com still needs further work to develop it. We have been working hard to encourage young people to read poetry by building up the Children's Poetry Bookshelf, running a national children's poetry competition for 7–11 year-olds and setting up a school shadowing scheme for the T. S. Eliot Prize in partnership with the English and Media Centre.

But all the time the idea of the PBS bringing poetry collections back into print kept niggling away, and finally we are launching the first fruit of our small reprint programme. Researching the list has made us realise just how much relatively recently published poetry is out of print. We don't feel that poems being made available in a *Collected*, meaning that they are technically in print, is quite the same thing, nor that it has the same appeal for readers. For publishers it is becoming harder to keep titles in print, because bookshops are not stocking a range of backlist stock. It's hard for publishers to reach potential book-buyers if the books cannot be sold into the shops.

Too many poets find their significant early collections have not been available for years and there is little prospect of them ever being brought back into print. The easy answer – using print on demand book production – is not one that all publishers will embrace. It may be more appealing in some cases to move towards an early *Selected* than to battle with the inertia that the book trade increasingly displays towards backlist poetry titles.

Working through the wide range of *Back in Print* suggestions from our members with Fiona Sampson has been an enjoyable experience. We're delighted to be able to make such first-rate writing available again and to enable readers to rediscover out-of-print favourites.

The titles chosen are:

Airy Hall by Fred D'Aguiar
Sibyls and Others by Ruth Fainlight
The Triumph of Love by Geoffrey Hill
Spilt Milk by Sarah Maguire
The Cost of Seriousness by Peter Porter
Adventures with My Horse by Penelope Shuttle

The *Back in Print* titles are all priced at £9.99 and can be ordered from the PBS online bookshop www.poetrybookshoponline.com or from the PBS direct, tel + 44 (0) 20 7833 9247. They can also be ordered through bookshops from the publication date of 29 January 2007.

Chris Holifield is the Director of the Poetry Book Society.

EDITORIAL

FIONA SAMPSON

As befits an issue published at the turn of the year, this quarter's *Poetry Review* looks both forwards and back, celebrating both new and existing work. Its theme of research, of excavation, may be nothing new after Heaney's 'Digging'; but in practice it can be challenging.

Publishing is an intuitive, unsystematized activity, often seeming disproportionately reliant on individual flair. Scholarly work in the field of contemporary British poetry – though undeniably serious – may be spread so thin as to produce primarily a map of individual passions. Reputations do form, albeit like silt against a groyne. But – how to excavate a pile of sand without destroying it? Radical refiguring is easy; but how can we learn more about the existing shape of – let's call it *the beach* – in a way that doesn't dismantle it? The first and best way is of course simply by *reading back*. *À la recherche* highlights the PBS's *Back in Print* series, on which *PR* has collaborated; which allows contemporary access to important collections, now out of print, of the 70s, 80s and 90s. We also celebrate Michael Longley's first four decades in poetry, marking the publication of his *Collected Poems* with new work, an interview and review. Continuing the retrospective theme, elsewhere C. L. Dallat reveals the origins in 80s London of what we've called the *Workshop Gen*; Steven Matthews looks at Faber's reissued *Irish* and *Scottish* anthologies; elegies by Ruth Fainlight and Michael Longley accompany books under review; Eavan Boland, John Fuller and David Harsent explore poetry of nostalgia.

But, over the last decade, much best public practice of poetry in the UK – awards, commissions, education, performance, outreach, publications, career development – has been generated by a single extraordinary protagonist. Until November 2006, Gary McKeone was Director of Literature at the Arts Council of England. As *PR* said, in a letter to ACE, when restructuring was announced, Gary "has a profoundly embedded knowledge of this country's contemporary literature – across genres and practices, from high literary publication to the widest community access programmes [and] he is, uniquely, as inspiring in his passion and insight into literary content as he is pragmatic and skilled at strategic administration". ACE promise in their response that "there is absolutely no truth in the suggestion made in some quarters that these changes represent a downgrading of literature within the Arts Council's work. The opposite is the case". Meanwhile, though, poetry readers need look neither far nor hard for evidence of Gary's professional generosity and literary intelligence. This issue of *PR* – itself supported by ACE – is for you, Gary.

NEWS FROM THE BEAT

LEMN SISSAY

It's a long haul flight from one terminal to another: Vancouver to London. *Long haul? Terminal?* Is it just me or is there something of The Darkness, something of The Final Metaphor, about these terms?

I am sat next to a Scottish grandmother and her delectable grand-daughter, Matilda, is perched between us. With two pirouetting pigtails Matilda looks precocious. She isn't precocious. She's an absolute sweetheart. But Grandmother Helen has the habit of speaking at me and not listening to my replies. *Long haul.* Having spent much of my childhood in Lochinver with a grandfather by the name of Duncan Munro I have more of a sense of Helen than she chooses to know. "So where are you from in Africa?" comes her question. All very interesting as questions go – should she have listened to my answer. "Yes," she says, before I finish my reply, "I once knew some Africans, nice people". *Terminal.* After being stuffed with airport food like a baby in a high chair, a few hours later comes this announcement.

"He's a poet," Helen coos at her granddaughter and then to everyone else on the plane. "A poet". We leave Vancouver at night, two hours late, and Helen's voice has softened. "Look at the lights Lemn – Lemn they're like," she pauses, "Like jewels in a jewellery box". I think, as I peer through the window, that all the lights in Vancouver make it look like I am above a sea of molten lava. It is a trick of the eye that I enjoy on night flights. An hour and I am asleep – until I open an eye to find an Air Hostess staring, very close to my face, in absolute silence. Helen is sleeping and Matilda, though playing with a Paddington bear – or, as Helen might have it, "Patrick the brave heart warrior bear" – is also staring. I wake with a start.

The Air Hostess's mouth preceded the question with a perfect pouting O. And then, aghast, "So what does a poet do?" she asks as we weave the sky. *Turbulence*, the title of Moira Dooley's book, comes to mind. *We do turbulence.* I break into a light sweat. The air hostess switches on the overhead light. "What does a poet do?" There's something of the interrogation about this. Through the clouds we swish, like the plane's an errant sewing machine from Hogwarts stitching the cloth. *We do turbulence and sky and everything below and above.*

I am on my way from one literature festival to another: from Arizona to Calgary to Banff to Vancouver and finally back to England and Poetry International. I feel like one of those old school TV map graphics would more aptly explain it. Those that show stitch marks for journeys. Or maybe a skipping stone splashing across the Atlantic making ripples in each city then skidding off to the next…

"Yes," Helen wakes, her eyes opening. The question has formed strange ripples on her forehead that read "What does a poet do?" Various answers come to mind. Make tea. Drink Alcohol. Make tea with alcohol. Avoid writing poems. Cling to poems. Sleep with poems. Divorce poems. Clean the apartment. Have tea with other poets and drink alcohol alone. Drink alcohol with other poets and make tea alone. Stay up late. Get up late. All these options and a thousand more come to mind. I contemplate whether to run off the more impressive elements of my biog but stop. After all, describing oneself in the third person is never as attractive as it is as an idea. Indeed it is unattractive. Ah, the biog – a thing of ugly beauty. In truth I avoid saying the most obvious and most profound and truthful answer – he writes poetry – and opt for the more worldly, "I do readings".

The Air Hostess – Air Steward as they are now known – is shocked. "You. Do. Readings". *This is a sign* she thinks and slowly, nervously and reverentially looking down at the palms of her hands she watches them uncurl as if the spirit was taking her. Her palms like two autumn leaves unfurling on a hand lotion advert. She stares at me with an expression of *this was meant to be*. She splays them towards me and with a look of true earnest says, "Will you read mine?"

It takes a split second for the penny to drop. "Will you read mine…". Not being one to disappoint I peer reluctantly at her hands, like an old pro, as if peeping over the edge of something. "You'll have to take that ring off so I can read them." I nod as if consumed. "Ahhh ahhhh," I say, as if coming across revelations. I follow the "Ahhh" with a sage "Yes, yes," and cock my head to the side. "What," she says, "What what…?". I study the hand a little harder. "You will meet a man on a plane, a poet…".

And there, dear reader, is the damning metaphor for the pitfalls of performing poetry – as soon as it puts the audience first it becomes a sham. I *write* poetry.

Lemn Sissay is Poet in Residence at Poetry International.

Frank Dullaghan
The Royal Academy

I'm taking my poem to be judged at the Royal Academy.
I'm taking it on the train. It's here on the seat beside me

wrapped in brown paper. Originally, I'd intended something large.
But that's been done so well, anything now would be a poor copy.

The train lurches through the suburbs – back gardens all stain and grime,
washed-out ochres, smoky greys. My poem sits quietly.

Perspective and composition have given way to ideas.
I'm taking the idea of my poem to be judged at the Royal Academy.

I've been thinking about it, here in the train beside me,
touching it up as the train enters into the dream

of backyards and walls, windows curtained with newspapers,
words catching the sun behind glass, browning.

It's always the dream that we want. I'm taking the dream of my poem
to the Royal Academy as the train leaves the tracks

and the houses gather up their lean-tos and sheds, their rusting bikes,
and peel away from the carriage window. We're together

as the sky rushes down and cloud presses its dead-flesh palms
to the glass. I'm being taken to the Royal Academy.

Dressed in brown paper, I'm holding something
tight and small, like a word not yet written.

I'm holding something for the judges. I'm holding something
that will subvert the walls of the Royal Academy.

Letter to the Editor

Like anyone else with a claw stuck in this odd world of poetry, I receive many unsolicited invitations to submit to competitions. All without exception stipulate a maximum number of lines, usually around forty. Why are there no competitions (that I am aware of) for longer poems?

I realise that the objection would be raised that it would take too much of a judge's time. But anyone who has worked as a script editor knows that, if certain characteristics are not in place very quickly, there is no point in reading further. It might also be objected that, as the main purpose of competitions is to raise money, there being few long poems, opening to these would defeat the purpose. That would be a more realistic obstacle[...] but one could always demand a higher entrance fee. Why not, please, at least in some instances remove the line length limit altogether? Or at least make it as ample as is generally the case with, for example, short story competitions.

GLYN HUGHES, SOWERBY BRIDGE

༃

Again, Please!

Poetry Review would like to hear more of …

There's no point imitating

Dennis O'Driscoll's *Poetry Pickings and Choosings* is a regular feature of *Poetry Ireland Review*. The contemporaneity of the quotes makes for always-absorbing reading; as do its teasing matches and mismatches. Sometimes it's like listening-in on a passionate pub argument, the one we all think we're in, where no-one's drunk and repeating themselves and every line is brilliant. O'Driscoll captures, in other words, something of the cutting edge of opinion as it's being formed. Rather than falling back on tried and tested maxims, his riskier practice mimics thought in action:

selecting, juxtaposing, sometimes even opposing, statements from criticism, journalism, poems and blogs.

Now he's brought the same technique to bear in *The Bloodaxe Book of Poetry Quotations* (2006, £9.95): which turns out to be an un-put-downable collection of quotations by and about poets and critics, on themes as various as 'Pushy Poets', 'Musical Arrangements' and – a favourite, this – 'Death by Poetry'. Often funny, frequently inspiring, always illuminating – it's a book which, in the hands of a lesser compiler, could have been just a stocking-filler. Instead, it's a surprising *vade mecum* for anyone concerned with the struggle to articulate what poetry does. Especially good is the comment-less juxtaposition. We particularly enjoyed, for example, tracing the lineage of the "I always say I'm a tax inspector" line (pp. 68-9). Given his own day job, we suggest, O'Driscoll may have enjoyed it even more...

Verse with purpose

At the start of every event at London's Poetry International this year, instead of a predicatable announcement about mobile phones, the ever-exuberant Lemn Sissay came rhyming over the loudspeakers:

> When the ring tone of a lone mobile phone
> Is the only lonely sound around
> And starts in the middle of
> Something funny or profound,
> The concentration constricts,
> It's an ill timed theatrical cough.
> It might be wise at the beginning of this
> To turn your mobile off.

'Mobile' was commissioned by the South Bank Centre during Lemn's residency at Poetry International 2006.

Poetry fortunes

In an often-demanding profession, who can resist poetry fortune cookies, first tasted at the Sha'ar Arabic-Hebrew festival and, on National Poetry Day, in our own Poetry Café...?

ॐ

CONTRIBUTORS

Amanda Aizpuriete is a Latvian poet. She has translated the works of many important 20th century writers and poets, most recently Akhmatova.

Eavan Boland's *New and Collected Poems* was reviewed in *PR 96:3*. This poem was first published in the *New Republic*.

Sean Borodale has held Fellowships at the Wordsworth Trust and the Rijksakakademie van beeldende kunst Amsterdam. He teaches at the Slade School of Art.

Alison Brackenbury is a poet, critic and writer for radio. *Singing in the Dark* is due from Carcanet in 2008.

Alan Brownjohn's *Collected Poems*, published this year, is reviewed on pp. 86-8.

Julia Casterton's *The Doves of Finisterre* won the Aldeburgh Jerwood Prize in 2004. She was recently awarded an Arts Council of England bursary.

C.L. Dallat reviews for the *Guardian, TLS* and BBC R4's *Saturday Review*. His latest collection is *Morning Star* (Lagan, Belfast). 'Love on a Rock' won the 2006 Strokestown Competition.

Greg Delanty's *Collected Poems 1986-2006* (Carcanet, 2006) was reviewed in PR *96:3*.

Frank Dullingham appears for the first time in *Poetry Review*.

Marie Étienne was born in Viet Nam. She is the author of twelve collections, three memoirs, a novel and studies of contemporary theatre. This sequence is from *Roi des cent cavaliers*, (Flammarion, 2002).

Ruth Fainlight's latest collection, *Moon Wheels* (Bloodaxe, 2006) was reviewed in *PR 96:3*. Her new translation of Sophocles's *Theban Plays*, done with Professor Robert Littman, will be brought out by Johns Hopkins University Press next year.

John Fuller's latest collection, *The Space of Joy* (Chatto, November 2006) is a PBS Recommendation.

Yvonne Green's poems have appeared in *London Magazine, Jewish Quarterly, The Wolf, Areté, Modern Poetry In Translation*, BBC Radio 4, etc.

Marilyn Hacker's latest collection is *Essays on Departure* (Carcanet, 2006).

David Harsent's *Legion* won the 2005 Forward Prize and was short-listed for the T.S. Eliot and Whitbread Prizes.

Alan Jenkins's most recent collection is *A Shorter Life*, short-listed for the 2005 Forward Prize.

Jackie Kay's latest collection is *Life Mask* (2005). In 2006 she was awarded an MBE for services to literature.

Michael Longley's *Collected Poems* is reviewed on pp. 79-81.

Christine De Luca writes in both her native Shetlandic and English. Her latest collection is *Parallel Worlds* (Luath Press, 2005).

E.A.Markham's fiction, *At Home with Miss Vanesa* (Tindal Street Press) was published in November 2006.

Glyn Maxwell's latest collection is *The Sugar Mile* (Picador, 2005). *The Nerve* (2002) won the Geoffrey Faber Memorial Prize.

Krystyna Milobędzka's collected poems, *Gathered 1960-2005*, appeared in Spring 2006.

David Morley's next collection of poetry is *The Invisible Kings* (Carcanet Press, 2007). He is Associate Professor at The University of Warwick where he directs the Warwick Writing Programme. *The Cambridge Introduction to Creative Writing* (CUP) is forthcoming.

Seán Ó Ríordáin (1916-77) was the first poet writing in Irish who merged Modernism with the Irish language tradition: his influence was seminal. He published four collections, one posthumous, and wrote a highly influential column for *The Irish Times*.

Ruth Padel has published six collections of poetry and been short-listed for the T.S.Eliot and Whitbread Prizes. *The Poem and the Journey* appears from Chatto in January 2007.

Alec Peever's latest project is *Art at the Centre* for Slough Borough Council.

Peter Porter's latest of more than twenty collections is *Afterburner* (Picador, 2004). He has the Queen's Gold Medal for Poetry.

Omar Sabbagh is at Goldsmith's College, London. He is a British/Lebanese poet with poems in the *Agenda Online Broadsheet* and *The Reader*.

Penelope Shuttle's eighth collection, *Redgrove's Wife* (2006) has been short-listed for the 2006 Forward and T.S.Eliot Prizes.

Shi Tao, poet and journalist, is serving ten years in a Chinese prison for having notified foreign media in 2004 of a government ban on commemorating the 1989 Tiananmen massacre.

Alys Tomlinson is a freelance photographer based in London and exhibiting internationally. She studied at Central Saint Martins College of Art. www.alystomlinson.co.uk

Jeffrey Wainwright's *Acceptable Words: Essays on the Poetry of Geoffrey Hill* was reviewed in *PR 96:2*.

John Weston, whose first collection *Chasing the Hoopoe* was published by Peterloo in 2005, worked in Beijing during Mao's Cultural Revolution.

Elżbieta Wójcik-Leese's translations of Marzanna Kielar are *Salt Monody* (Zephyr Press, USA, 2006).

Yang Lian's latest collection in English is *Concentric Circles* (Bloodaxe, 2005).